Internet Famous

A Practical Guide to
Becoming an Online Celebrity

By Cameron Chapman

Untime
Press
Orleans, VT
www.untimepress.com

Copyright

Visit our Web site at www.untimepress.com for more
information.

Chapman, Cameron.
Internet Famous: A Practical Guide to Becoming an Online
Celebrity / by Cameron Chapman.
ISBN-13:
1. 978-0-9825382-0-3

Cover images from sxc.hu.

About the Author

Cameron Chapman is a fulltime writer, blogger, and web designer. She's been writing about social media and Internet topics for more than two years for some of the most popular blogs in the world. She lives in northern New England but spends most of her time on Twitter (twitter.com/cameron_chapman) or Facebook.

Dedication

To my husband, Mike, who believed in this project from the start and has stood by me no matter what crazy ideas I come up with. Thank you.

Acknowledgements

There are a number of people who made this book possible. First I have to thank all of the wonderful members of Authonomy, who have created a place where a new writer can flourish and grow alongside those with more experience. My writing would not be where it is today if not for them.

While it would be impossible to thank everyone who has helped to make this book happen, I would like to thank the following people specifically for their contributions:

My father, John Chapman, who helped finance this book.

Dan Holloway, Jason Richard Horger, and George LaCas, who beta-read the first draft of this book and provided invaluable feedback. If not for them, this book would probably be unintelligible.

My mother, Diana Lopez, who proofread the book for me.

Leo Babauta of Zen Habits (http://zenhabits.net), who was kind enough to answer tons of questions for me and allowed the use of some of his blog content in this book.

Jason Tanz and Wired Magazine, who published an article about Julia Allison and becoming Internet Famous in their August 2008 issue, which inspired the creation of this book.

Table of Contents

Social Media

What the heck is it, really?

According to Wikipedia, "social media is information content created by people using highly accessible and scalable publishing technologies." Generally speaking, social media refers to Internet technologies that offer end-users the ability to interact and create content that is then shared with other users. Users can build an online identity that can (and often does) carry over from one platform to another.

The term "social media"—also referred to as "new media"—is broad-reaching and actually covers multiple kinds of online applications. They can be broken down into a number of different categories:

- Communications platforms such as blogging and social networking.
- Collaborative platforms like wikis and social news sites.
- Multimedia sites for sharing photos, videos, artwork, and more.
- Entertainment sites that include virtual worlds and online gaming communities.

- Review and opinion sites where you can offer advice or review products.

The biggest draw of social media sites is their ability to allow people to form personal and business relationships and have conversations with others who share common interests from around the world. There are communities in virtually every interest niche out there from arts and crafts to quantum physics. Sites allow users to share content and learn from each other, providing an invaluable resource for hobbyists and professionals alike.

A Brief History of Social Media

There were a few precursors to social media present throughout the 1980s and 1990s. One of these precursors was dating sites, which allowed users to display an online profile. Also included were ICQ and AIM, which allowed users to create lists of friends, and BBSs, which allowed users who were previously unknown to each other to connect online and discuss common interests.

The first recognizable social media site was the now-defunct SixDegrees.com. Founded in 1997, it was the first site that allowed users to create profiles and publicly list their friends. At one point the site boasted more than a million members. Though it closed in 2001, SixDegrees.com was an important forerunner to social networking sites still in operation today.

In 1999, LiveJournal was started as the first community blogging platform. LiveJournal users were and are still encouraged to network with other users. Connections with others are displayed on their profiles, creating a true social network in addition to the blogging platform. Also started that year was competing blog network, Blogger (Blogspot).

Friendster was founded in 2002 and quickly grew in popularity among three key groups: bloggers, Burning Man festival attendees, and gay men. Before press coverage began in 2003, there were already more than 300,000 active users on the network.

2003 brought the launches of MySpace, LinkedIn, and Last.fm, all of which are still popular. MySpace grew rapidly on rumors that Friendster would become a fee-based service. Indie rock bands who were banned from Friendster for profile regulation violations were some of MySpace's earliest adopters and musicians (and their fans) continue to be some of its most active users. In 2004, MySpace started gaining popularity with teenagers and embraced the underage population (unlike most of their predecessors, who insisted users be 18 or older). When MySpace was purchased in 2005 by News Corporation for $580 million, mainstream media coverage of the growing site was overwhelming and privacy and safety issues became a problem, particularly for users younger than 18.

In 2004, Facebook launched as a Harvard-only niche social networking site (users had to have a Harvard.edu email address to join). It soon began supporting other schools, but still required users to have a .edu email address. The following year they expanded to include high school students and then professionals within corporate networks. Eventually, Facebook became open to everyone and is now one of the most popular general social networking sites in existence.

Blog networks and platforms were also becoming popular in the early 2000s, with Movable Type starting in 2001 and WordPress starting in 2003. Other notable social media startups in the early 2000s were DeviantART (2000), an online community for artists working in a variety of media; Wikipedia (2001), an open source, user-edited encyclopedia; Meetup.com (2002), a site devoted to helping those with common interests connect and meet each other in the "real world"; and PBWiki (2003), a "wiki farm" where users can start their own topical wikis.

The mid-2000s brought the advent of online media sharing. Flickr, the photo-sharing network, got its start in 2004. YouTube,

Google Video, and blip.tv all came on the scene the following year. Twitter, the first microblogging platform, was launched in 2006. The mid-2000s also brought a wave of specialized social networks, including niche networks for farmers; Ning, a site that allows you to start your own niche social network; Stylefeeder, a social network devoted to fashion; and sisterwoman.com, a social network for feminists.

Social networks and social media have continued to grow and show no signs of slowing down. User numbers are up every day, with MySpace currently leading the way with more than 250,000,000 users and Facebook with more than 175,000,000. WordPress.com currently boasts almost 150,000 bloggers (not including those who have self-hosted WordPress on their own servers). LiveJournal has had more than 19.3 million journals and communities formed since they began in 1999.

Filling a Need

Successful social media sites fill the needs of a group of Internet users. Whether the need they seek to fulfill is shared by a large portion of those online or by a select few, they all meet the needs of someone.

Take Facebook, for example. At Harvard, each House had it's own "face book" (like a yearbook) but there was no universal, campus-wide version. So Mark Zuckerberg started one on his own in February of 2004. It quickly grew from being a Harvard-only site to including students from Stanford, Columbia and Yale, and then eventually to all the Ivy League schools and those in the Boston area. But the initial need was a campus-wide directory of sorts, somewhere students could look up the photos of other students (or the names of students they'd seen around campus).

YouTube was started after its founders had difficulty sharing videos online with each other. YouTube has grown to be the largest video-sharing site online, based on basic need fulfillment.

No matter what social media site you look at, it's likely the founders identified a specific need that wasn't being filled (or wasn't being filled adequately) and then developed a way to fill it. In many cases these sites have evolved past their original need-fulfillment, but they wouldn't have existed in the first place if it hadn't been for that initial lack.

Similarities and Differences Between Social Media and Traditional Media

Traditional media, otherwise referred to as industrial media, are generally those things we traditionally think of as "The Media"—newspapers, magazines, television, and radio. CNN, NBC, Hearst, the *New York Times*, *The Wall Street Journal*, Sirius, XM, CBS. They're also the local TV network affiliates, local newspapers, local magazines, local radio stations. These are the media outlets that have been around for as long as most of us can remember. They're part of our daily lives, either because we actively consume them or we see others doing so.

But social media is different. Instead of being strictly consumers, social media allows people to become *producers*. Social media provides tools for anyone with Internet access to distribute their own content to anyone who will listen. It changes the dynamic by removing many of the barriers to entry that traditional media have always had.

The main similarity between traditional media and social media is their ability to reach an audience spread all over the world. Traditional media primarily accomplishes this through a lot of money and established infrastructure systems (printing presses, television and radio broadcasting equipment, supply chains, and similar things). Social media, by comparison, is based largely on inexpensive technologies and an existing public infrastructure accessible to just about anyone.

Other major differences between social media and traditional media have to do with the control of information. Magazines, newspapers, and television and radio stations, along with other traditional media sources are expensive to operate and therefore limit who can own them. Social media, on the other hand, is inherently inexpensive and easy to use, allowing virtually anyone with an Internet connection to provide news, information, and opinion to anyone else with an Internet connection.

Social media technologies can be learned by almost anyone. Free tutorials exist for all aspects of computer and Internet usage, including blogging, social networking, digital photography, video creation, and more. Traditional media often requires much more specialized training, which usually requires a large investment in terms of both time and money.

In increasing numbers, breaking news is being released on social networking sites before being covered by traditional news outlets. Part of this stems from having active users all over the world; there's a good chance one of them will be an eyewitnes to breaking news and report it on sites like Twitter, often linked with photos.

Major Social Media Players

There are leaders in each sector of the social media industry. From MySpace and Facebook in the social networking sphere to YouTube for video and Digg for social news, each kind of social media has its major players. Of course, there are plenty of niche sites with their own loyal followings and communities, too.

Blogs

WordPress. Blogger. Movable Type. TypePad. LiveJournal. Tumblr. There's a blogging platform out there suitable for just about anyone. Blogger, Tubmlr, and LiveJournal are free blogging communities that host your blog for you. TypePad does the same but is a paid service (and is built on the Movable Type platform). Movable Type is an open source platform with both free and paid licenses (depending on use) that you host on your own server. WordPress offers both hosted (WordPress.com) and self-hosted (WordPress.org) platforms. All of the above platforms can be extended through plugins and widgets.

Microblogging

Twitter is the leading microblogging platform. Ping.fm is another similar service, though they send out your messages to whichever social networking site you choose (including Twitter).

Social Networking

Facebook and MySpace are the leading general social networks. LinkedIn is the leading social network for business. There are hundreds of other niche social networks out there for everyone from farmers to feminists. And building new social networks is becoming easier every day. Sites like Ning set up everything for you and host your network with both free and paid packages. Open source software is also available, including the Buddy Press plugin set for WordPress MU (a multi-user version of WordPress). Social networks are a major part of any campaign to become Internet famous.

Social Network Aggregation

With so many social networks available, efforts have been made to integrate the information you may include on one site with every other site you're actively involved with. Applications like Gravatar offer a unified avatar (profile photo) across platforms, linked to your email address. FriendFeed collects your activities across more than forty different sites, including Flickr and YouTube, and makes them available on your other profiles (like Facebook).

Social Bookmarking

Tracking interesting information you find online and sharing it with others is another useful way to make yourself known. It's also a great way to promote your own content to others. Sites like Del.icio.us and StumbleUpon are useful for not only keeping track of things you find interesting, but also for promoting your own articles, videos, and other content.

Social News

Social news sites like Digg and Reddit are another way of getting your content out to the masses. Making the front page of Digg can send tens of thousands of visitors to your site in a single day and, if you make it there often enough, bring you from Internet oblivion to Internet stardom.

Photo Sharing

Flickr is the most socially-active photo sharing site out there. There are groups and photo pools for just about every imaginable topic (even topics you probably wouldn't think of as particularly photogenic). Photos can be released on the site under a variety of Creative Commons licensing options (or with regular Copyright protections), making it a valuable resource not only for promoting and distributing your own photos, but also for finding photos to use on your blog or website.

Video Sharing

YouTube is the most popular video-sharing site out there. Users can create channels to promote their own videos. It's a valuable platform for getting your message out and can bring tons of traffic to your website, blog, and anywhere else you may choose if used in the right manner. Other major players in the video sharing sphere are Revver and Google Video.

Podcasting and Vlogging

Podcasting is basically audio blogging. Vlogging is video blogging. Any video sharing site can be used for vlogging, including YouTube. iTunes is popular for distributing podcasts, as is odea, which has an imbeddable MP3 player you can use for distributing your podcast through your blog.

Lifecasting

Lifecasting is similar to video sharing, but done live. Sites like Justin.tv, Ustream.tv, and BlogTV offer platforms for doing live video sessions and video chats. Skype is also sometimes used for lifecasting.

Wikis

Wikis provide opportunities for disseminating information. Because wikis are generally moderated by large groups of users, the information contained on them is usually accurate (though newly added information may be suspect). Wikipedia is the most well-known wiki but there are other niche wikis out there for almost any subject. And there are platforms like WetPaint and PBWiki that let you easily create your own topical wiki.

What You Need to Know

- Spend some time researching the different social media offerings available.
- Brainstorm about ways you could use each social media technology outlined above.
- Keep reading for more information about each of the technologies outlined here.
- Stay on the lookout for new social media technologies, as new ones are constantly being developed.

Internet Famous
Better than real-life famous!

I nternet famous means just what it says: being well-known online. Whether it's in a single niche community or across the web in general, the Internet famous have a certain amount of name recognition online. Sometimes this translates into becoming well-known in the "real world"—the world of the mainstream media.

Types of Internet Famous

Some people are Internet famous just for being themselves (kind of like Paris Hilton became famous just for being Paris Hilton), or at least a version of themselves (like Julia Allison or iJustine). Others are famous for a product they're associated with, either online or off (like Pete Cashmore of the blog Mashable or Tim Ferriss, author of the book *The 4-Hour Workweek*). Each type of Internet fame has its own advantages and drawbacks.

If your main goal is to become Internet famous to promote a product you're selling, you'll need to take a slightly different approach than if you just want to be famous for fame's sake. If your goal is Internet fame to push yourself for some professional aspiration, that also requires a different set of techniques. If all you want is to be recognized, your options are somewhat more open, as you don't have as much to worry about in terms of negative publicity carrying over to your professional sphere (feel free to live by the phrase "any publicity is good publicity"). Just be aware that employers often keep tabs on what their employees are doing online, even when it's unrelated to their work, and are sometimes firing or reprimanding employees based on their online behavior.

Famous for Being Yourself (or Some Version of Yourself)

Gaining fame for being yourself is probably the more difficult of the two methods for becoming Internet famous. You need to come up with an angle for yourself, something that sets you apart from your peers. Maintaining a consistent persona can also be a problem, depending on how far from your true personality you stray. To some extent, you'll need to focus on creating a caricature of your real self. Figuring out an angle and following through with it is the best way to propel yourself to the forefront of Internet fame.

In order to gain Internet fame just for being yourself, you'll need to be willing to put yourself out there. Share the good and the bad in your life. And be honest with your readership. Dishonesty and lies are very easily revealed online, especially as your fame grows. As you become more well-known, it's almost a given that you'll have detractors hunting for things to use against you. Don't give them any extra ammo if you can help it.

Justine Ezarik, better known as iJustine, is a lifecaster who shares her entire life online through videos on Justin.tv. She's best known for an online video she produced discussing her 300-page iPhone bill in August of 2007 that quickly went viral, gaining more than 3 million views in just 10 days. Largely due to that video, AT&T changed their iPhone billing policies.

But that video wasn't the beginning of Justine's push for online celebrity. She'd already been lifecasting on Justin.tv since May 29, 2007 and was the first person on the site to have her own lifecasting channel (other than founder Justin Kan).

Famous for a Product

Becoming famous for a product is a bit more clear-cut than becoming famous just for being you. You'll still need to portray a consistent persona but you don't necessarily need to reveal as much about yourself and your life when you're pushing a product. You will need to look for ways to branch out and you'll likely need to give something away in order to get maximum publicity.

Giving away content is one of the best ways to gain publicity, especially if you make it feel like an exclusive offer. This is why an ebook will sometimes be more successful than a simple blog. Putting up barriers to entry, even if they're arbitrary or not really difficult, make people feel like they're part of an elite group.

Offering unique information on your site is another way to spur interest. Spreading your content over multiple channels (your blog, social networks, microblogging, etc.) is another good way to increase interest and get your fans more involved.

Timothy Ferriss, author of The 4-Hour Work Week, used the blogosphere to launch his book and quickly push it to number one on the New York Times Bestseller list. By contacting and conversing with bloggers, he gained free publicity for his book and became an Internet celebrity before quickly gaining mainstream media attention. According to his website, he's been featured by more than a hundred media outlets, including *Time*, *Forbes*, the *New York Times*, *The Economist* and more. He continues to maintain his Internet presence through his own blog, Twitter, the *Huffington Post*, and *Wired* magazine.

The Internet Infamous

If fame is your only goal, the Internet is a great place to get it. Doing something crazy, unexpected, or stupid is much more likely to go viral and get widespread attention. Posting a video on YouTube and then linking to it wherever you can is one way to get publicity. If your video is crazy enough or unique enough, your friends and acquaintances are more likely to pass it on. Remember, too, that one of the best ways to get people to share your link or content is simply to ask.

The same thing can happen when something you were doing with the intention of getting positive publicity (or even no publicity) backfires. This could be blogging about your employer and then getting fired for it, or posting things about your family and dealing with the backlash from it. It could be a video you thought was completely serious that everyone else takes as a joke (or vice versa). Make sure when embarking on a campaign to become Internet famous that you're willing to make the most of whatever comes your way, and make sure you have a thick skin.

Pioneers of Being Internet Famous

We've already mentioned Justine Ezarik, one of the pioneers of lifecasting (more about that in Chapter 11). One of the most famous bloggers out there is Robert Scoble, whose blog, Scobleizer, came into the limelight while he was an evangelist for Microsoft. In 2005, Scobel became the first person to be called a "spokesblogger" because of his positive coverage of Microsoft (even though he often criticized the company and praised its competitors, including Apple). In 2007, Scoble joined Fast Company where he still works.

Pete Cashmore is another Internet celeb who gained fame because of his blog, Mashable, The Social Media Blog. Mashable was started from his bedroom in Scotland in 2005 as a way to keep track of new social media startups and quickly became a startup in itself, growing to be one of the most popular blogs on the Internet and the most popular one devoted to social media. He's been featured in *Business Week* and as one of the Forbes Top 25 Internet Celebrities of 2007. Because of the focus of Mashable, it's not surprising that Cashmore has accounts on virtually every major social media site out there, (Twitter, Facebook, LinkedIn, Flickr, MySpace, and FriendFeed for starters) though many of them are listed under "Mashable" instead of his name.

Julia Allison is probably one of the best-known Internet celebs out there. She took a slightly different approach to gaining Internet fame by associating herself with celebrities and public figures and making sure photos of herself with them were distributed far and wide online. She also maintains at least three blogs, a video blog, Twitter account, and Facebook fan page among other social media accounts.

Reasons to be Internet Famous

Internet fame has definite advantages. If you love being the center of attention, Internet fame can keep you there 24/7. If you have a product to sell or a service to offer, becoming widely known online can convert into serious sales figures. Coverage from bloggers was a huge factor in catapulting Tim Ferriss' book, *The 4-Hour Workweek*, to the top of the *New York Times* bestseller list. Internet fame can often translate into real-life fame. Plenty of talk shows and news programs are looking for experts on various topics and they're turning to the Internet more and more often to find them. You could be one of those experts. And sometimes you can get mainstream media coverage just because of the sheer size of your Internet success

One of the biggest advantages of Internet fame compared to traditional fame is how easy it is for your fans and followers to take action. Whether you're selling a product or just yourself, the Internet makes it easy for people to do what you ask. When something is featured in the mainstream media, instant action isn't always possible. Asking someone to go to a website when they're reading a magazine is less likely to get results. Unless they're sitting right at their computer, there's a good chance by the time they are it will be forgotten. Even with the advent of handheld devices capable of browsing the Internet, there's still a slim chance they'll interrupt what they're doing and go to the website mentioned immediately. But when all you're asking is to click a link, it makes action that much easier. And that translates into more people doing what you're asking of them.

Converting Internet Fame into Real Life Fame

Once you've built up a following for yourself, be on the lookout for traditional media opportunities. Television shows and magazines often put out an editorial calendar days, weeks, or even months prior to covering a specific topic. If there's something coming up that fits your area of expertise, pitch yourself as a good article of interview candidate. Cold-calling media outlets to pitch yourself or your story is also an option. Don't underestimate local media, either. Journalists often scan local papers for stories that might be appropriate for larger news audiences, whether in print or on TV or radio shows.

Open Up Opportunities for Yourself

Opportunities for product endorsements, book deals, and other paid gigs can open up based on your Internet fame. Once you're a celebrity in your niche, you're more likely to have offers coming your way. But there's no reason you can't seek them out on your own. Pitch a book to an agent or publishing house. Pitch an article or series of articles to a national magazine in your niche. Put up notices on your website that you're looking for joint promotional opportunities. Seek interviews on television and radio shows to get your name out there to a wider audience. If you're funny enough or have a strong enough personality, it may lead to a more regular radio or television gig.

Sell a Product or Draw Attention to Your Business or Organization

If your goal is to sell a product, make sure you mention that product wherever you can. Seek out attention from media outlets whose readers, viewers, or listeners are members of your target market. Using search engine optimization (SEO) and connecting within niche communities that appeal to your idea customer are key to selling your product. Developing connections and trust within those communities prior to pitching your product are also key to making a bigger impact. If you just come in pitching a product, you're less likely to get a welcoming response. In fact, many communities can be downright hostile to new members who start right out pitching a product or service.

Pitching yourself to bloggers and other online influencers is another valuable way of getting publicity. Guest-blogging or syndicating articles is another great way to get your name out there and helps to establish you as an expert (and including a link to your website or blog brings you more traffic).

Draw Attention to a Cause

Maybe it's not attention for yourself that you're after. If there's a cause you're passionate about, whether it's endangered species or women's rights or anything in-between, gaining Internet fame can lead to raising awareness for your cause. If you're passionate about stopping global warming, start an environmental blog. If you're passionate about women's rights in third-world countries, start a blog covering charities that help them or, if you're an avid traveler, showcasing your first-hand experiences in those countries (a photoblog would work really well for the latter).

Don't be afraid to make a fool of yourself in support of your cause. Sometimes doing something a bit off-the-wall can lead to more traffic and more awareness. Just keep in mind that the things you do online reflect on your cause. Don't do anything that could be construed as negative or offensive, or you risk harming the charities you're trying to help.

What You Need to Know

- Internet fame can be just as powerful as fame in traditional media outlets, and sometimes even more so.
- There are many reasons for seeking Internet fame, from wanting to promote a product to wanting to promote a cause to just wanting to promote yourself.
- Different social media platforms are more or less suited to different kinds of fame.
- Internet fame has some definite advantages over traditional, mainstream media fame.

Your Niche

Why you have to have one!

Your best bet for gaining Internet fame is to focus on a single niche topic or audience. Tailoring your personality and your efforts toward one group of people increases your likelihood of success. The other big benefit to working on just one niche is that there's less competition—there are fewer people trying to get attention.

Even if you want to build up a reputation among different groups of people, your best bet is to focus on one at a time. Focusing in on one group or niche at a time means you're less likely to stretch yourself too thin and more likely that your efforts will be fruitful.

What Are You Passionate About?

To start selecting your niche, make a list of things you're interested in and things that hold a prominent place in your daily life. Whether it's cars or kids or cats or clothes, you probably have tons of diverse interests and activities in your life. List every one you can think of for starters. Just including them on your list opens up your options and sometimes one idea can spur another. Write down anything that comes to mind, regardless of what it is (we'll get to that later). Mind-mapping can be helpful for doing this, too.

Once you have your list, look it over and cross anything off that you find embarrassing or too personal to write about publicly. Cross off anything you think you might lose interest in over the next year or two (Internet fame is a long-term commitment). And cross off anything you think you might get sick of if you spent every day dealing with it. Your finished list should have at least a dozen niches still listed when you finish this (and hopefully no more than a couple dozen).

Finding a Low-Competition Niche

When your list has been whittled down to only those things you're really interested in, it's time to do a little research. You need to find out which niche has the most traffic with as few established, popular personalities as possible. A niche like technology or computers is going to be much harder to break into because there are so many established players. The same thing goes for fashion or cars or making money online. They've all been done over and over and they all have their established celebrities.

But choosing something more specialized, either a sub-topic of any of the above (men's fashion is one area where there aren't a whole lot of online celebrities, though there is plenty of competition from traditional media sources), means there's less competition. While the audience numbers might be lower in a more limited niche, breaking into the collective consciousness of its followers is easier. Competing with a hundred established online celebrities for a million readers is a lot tougher than competing with five well-known personalities for a hundred thousand readers. And in the latter case, you may end up with more readers overall than you would have in the first place.

Passion is the most important thing you can bring to any topic you choose. If you're not passionate about your subject, it will come through in your writing. Being able to generate enthusiasm on a daily basis for something is not easy if you don't love what you're doing. In the real world, those who only care about making money are often the ones who fail miserably at any business they pursue. Those who are passionate about what they're doing, on the other hand, can often overcome huge odds to become successful, even if everyone thought they'd fail. The same holds true online.

If you're pushing an established product, your niche options won't be as open as someone who's either pushing themselves or doesn't yet have a product. But finding a unique angle for pushing your product can make the difference between finding only a handful of fans and becoming Internet famous. Identifying your target customer is a good place to start. Once you know who they are and what they're interested in, you can tailor your efforts toward their specific online activities.

Now, if you're trying to be famous just for yourself and not to push a product or cause, you might be thinking, "I don't need a niche." Nothing could be further from the truth. But finding your niche will be a bit different. Think about who you want your fans to be. Teenagers? Fashionistas? Techies? Gamers? Musicians? Baby boomers? Once you know who you want to appeal to, you can think about the kinds of things they're interested in and the types of social media they use. With that information in hand, you can tailor your promotional efforts to reaching those people. You can't be all things to all people. Just as real-life celebrities often appeal to one demographic or another (athletes appeal to sports fans and horror book authors don't try to appeal to those who are afraid of their own shadow), Internet celebrities should do the same.

Make sure you don't choose a niche that's going to be difficult to keep up on. If you live in northern Minnesota, it's going to be difficult to cover celebrity news. You're unlikely to ever get the scoop on something because, let's face it, there aren't a whole lot of celebrities hanging out in northern Minnesota. The same goes for just about any topic where getting the scoop on something or inside information is the best way to success. If you don't live near the epicenter of an industry or at least have contacts within that industry, it's going to be that much harder to get any traction. That's not to say it's impossible, just that you're setting yourself up for a lot more challenges if you don't at least consider these issues.

Finding a High-Demand Niche

Maybe you've got a couple of niches you're considering but can't make up your mind between them. One thing to consider is how much traffic a niche is likely to generate. The more mainstream your niche, the higher the traffic numbers are likely to be (but competition is likely higher, too). A sub-niche is often the way to go (ie, instead of fashion, you could cover men's or children's fashion; instead of cars, you could cover muscle cars or drift cars). The more traffic, the more potential fans are available.

There are plenty of free tools available to find out search volume. Reading websites that follow online trends and buzz are great places to start to find a popular topic. Watch what seems to be consistently popular. Try to pick out which are just fads and which are long-term trends. A lot of these sites and services offer trend graphs that show traffic and interest over previous weeks or months.

Try Things Out

If you're unsure of which niche you want to pursue, you have a few different options. You can always start multiple blogs or campaigns to see which one seems to pan out quicker. Try starting a blog or two on a free blog host and see what kind of traffic you get without a whole lot of effort. If one seems to be taking off a lot easier than the other, or if you find yourself growing sick of a topic after only a couple of weeks, then you'll have a better idea of which niche is most suitable to you.

Another option is to try asking around on social networks and microblogs to see if there's much interest in one or another of your potential topics. Delve deeper into your topic research to see what's lacking. Then theorize about why it might be lacking. Is it because there's just not enough interest? Because your target audience doesn't care about that kind of thing? Or is it just because no one's tried it yet?

While you can usually find an audience for just about any topic online, make sure the niche you're after has enough people interested in it to achieve your goals. Some people will be happy if a few hundred people know who they are and consider them an expert. Others won't be happy unless thousands or even millions of people know who they are. Either one is fine. Just make sure your chosen niche can support your aims.

Finding Resources Specific to Your Niche

Search engines are the logical place to start when you're looking for information on a specific niche. Technorati, Google Blog Search, and other blog directories are another great place. Search for "top rated blogs" or "most popular blogs" (with or without keywords specific to your niche) to get lists of the most popular blogs online.

Finding the Gatekeepers

Each niche has gatekeepers, the established sites with a long track record and a certain level of respect. Look for roundup posts within your niche. These often list blogs covering your topic along with other resources. Make note of which blogs and sites (or specific people) are mentioned often in posts related to your niche. Then check out the popularity of those sites using Google Page Rank, Alexa, Quantcast, Technorati and other metrics sites.

Once you've found the most popular blogs and experts within your niche, see if there's something missing from what they're covering. Consider angles you could use to gain popularity. Spend some time going through the archives of these other sites to see what their style is. Do they have a set editorial schedule? How often do they post? Do their writers post personal information and anecdotes or not? Keep notes on these things for future reference.

Making a list of useful blogs within your niche is very valuable. Linking to other blogs in your niche, even those that directly compete with you, is one part of gaining notoriety. As you make yourself a member of your niche's community, you're more likely to get links back to your own site from established blogs. Building up a name for yourself by being quoted on other useful sites is an important step in becoming Internet famous.

Creating a Personality That Fits Within Your Niche

Once you've chosen your niche, you'll need to decide what personality will be best suited for gaining popularity within it. While I don't advise changing your personality completely or pretending to be someone you're not (unless, of course, your goal for Internet stardom is to become an actor), concentrating on one aspect of your personality can make you more accessible. Think of it in the same manner as you do the different personalities you project in your real life. You probably act one way at work (or school), one way with your family, and another way with your close friends. All are parts of your overall personality, but some parts are more appropriate for certain situations than other parts.

The best way to figure all this out is to think about what your target audience is looking for. If you're looking for professional recognition, you need to be professional in all of your dealings online. If you're looking for general Internet fame, you might want to portray yourself as a bit more off the wall or intense or, at least, more casual. If your goal is to promote a product, portray yourself as someone who uses or has been helped by that product. In other words, if you're selling an organizational system, you need to come across as organized. If you're selling clothing, wear your designs. If you're offering financial services, make sure you come across as someone who knows how to handle their own finances. Beware of how personal anecdotes come across and make sure they fit in with the image you're trying to portray.

Try to keep your online personality as close to your real-life personality as you can. Constantly having to put on an act becomes tiring. And the more your stray from who you truly are, the more likely you are to break character and act in a way that isn't consistent with what your fans are expecting.

Another thing to keep in mind is, what is going to be off limits? What are you not willing to share with complete strangers? For some Internet famous personalities, virtually everything is fair game, from bodily functions to family problems to money issues. Others only like to share things that are relevant to the product or service they're selling. Maybe you're uncomfortable sharing anything about your family or your day job. Maybe you have a hobby you'd like to keep just to yourself or particular reading habits you don't want to share. It's fine if there are things you'd rather keep private; just make sure you identify what they are up front and figure out ways to keep them out of your digital life if necessary. Remember, too, that information you broadcast online is accessible to anyone. Be wary about publishing personal information that might put you in danger, like when you're going on vacation or are home alone for an extended stretch. You never know who might be reading.

As your fame increases, keeping your personal life private may become harder, especially if you participate in industry events or other offline activities. Keeping some things private from the start makes it easier to maintain your privacy as your fame increases. Rumors are bound to crop up as your fame grows but, then again, sometimes rumors only serve to make you even more famous!

What You Need to Know

- Your best bet for gaining Internet fame is to choose a high-demand, low-competition niche.
- Once you've chosen a niche, customize your personality and your strategy for better results.
- Your niche combined with your unique personality are what set you apart from your competitors.
- Don't be afraid to keep some parts of your life private.
- As your fame grows, maintaining your privacy may become increasingly more difficult.
- Sometimes the rumor mill only serves to increase your fame.

Your Website

Social media-friendly web design 101

Your website is the starting point of your social media publicity campaign. While some people get by with just a profile on their social networking site(s) of choice, a website puts you a notch ahead of your competitors.

Your website doesn't need to be complex but it does need to be put together well. You need to take some time to plan out what you want from your site, the kinds of information you'll include, and the image you're trying to portray (this links back to your chosen personality, as discussed in Chapter 3).

One thing to consider is whether to design your own site or hire someone to do it for you. If you have the money and don't have much experience with web design, you may want to find someone who does, whether it's a professional or a friend. You'll save yourself a lot of headaches hiring a professional and a basic site generally won't cost more than a few hundred dollars. If you're more of a do-it-yourself kind of person, there are plenty of free resources online that can show you step-by-step how to design your own site.

Your Personal Brand

We're all familiar with brands and branding. We're bombarded with advertisements every day, on television, in magazines, on the radio, and online. And we often associate them with big corporations: Pepsi, Disney, Ikea, Ralph Lauren, and the like. But branding isn't just for the big shots. Creating a consistent image for yourself, your own personal brand, is a good way to increase your recognizability.

Your personal brand includes a few different elements. One element is your appearance and the appearance of things you're associated with (such as your website and blog). Another is your personality. Remember that your online activities give an impression about the type of person you are and what your personality is likely to be. Make sure these are in sync with what you want to portray. The most important part of your personal brand, though, is the bit that sets you apart from others in your niche. This is something that's unique to you. Whatever you choose to use as your differentiating point, it should be something that can't be easily replicated by your competitors.

Creating your own personal brand isn't that difficult. Start with using a single primary photo to use across your website, social media profiles, and other places where you have a presence. Next comes a color palette. There are tons of resources online for finding out the meanings behind different colors and additional tools are available to find a coordinating color palette.

From there it's a matter of personal taste. Read on for more information on individual elements you should consider when creating your website.

Your Own Domain

I can't stress this one enough: buy your own domain name! A domain name will cost you around $10 a year. Owning yourname. com or yourproduct.com is an investment in your future success.

Think of it this way: if you achieve your goals of Internet fame and you don't own your name as a domain, how long do you think it will be before someone else buys it? And then tries to charge you an arm and a leg to buy it back? While domain squatting (buying a domain containing someone else's trademark with the intent to resell it to them for a profit) is illegal, it might be hard to prove someone was doing that with your name (especially if your name is a common one or not particularly unique). If it's a product name it's often easier to prove someone is squatting but reclaiming your domain can still be time-consuming and costly.

You might consider registering both "yourname.com" and "yourname.net" domains. If your name is already taken (which it could be if it's common), consider other ways of incorporating your name into your domain combined with other words. One of Julia Allison's websites is located at "itsmejulia.com." It's an excellent example of using your name in a creative way that's also memorable.

What to Include

Deciding what to include on your website can be a very tough decision. Again, it's going to depend on what you're looking to get out of Internet fame. If your goal is to become famous just for yourself, then you may want to include a lot more personal information on your site than if you're pushing a product.

There are a few basics you'll likely want to include no matter what kind of fame you're seeking. First is a photo of yourself. No matter the reason you're seeking Internet fame, you're going to have to put yourself out there. Next is some kind of bio. Whether it's a full biography or just in relation to your professional life, you'll need to give your fans some information about who you are. The third component to include is a link to each of your other social media profiles and your blog (more on those in later chapters).

If your goal is to push a product or service, you'll want separate pages offering more details about them. Even if your product or service has its own website, providing at least one basic page is a good idea for search engine optimization purposes.

If your aim is to become famous in general, you'll want to include more information about yourself. Consider including a photo gallery, videos, articles, and a press kit. These guidelines also apply if you're promoting yourself in order to gain recognition for a cause.

A Unique Design

Whether you're designing your site yourself or having someone else do it, you want the site's design to be uniquely *you*. The colors, the layout, and the overall feel of the site needs to make people think of you when they see it. It needs to echo your brand and your persona.

Using Templates

If a unique design is so important, then why am I talking about using a template? Well, because templates are a great place to start, especially if you're not comfortable designing a website completely from scratch. Taking a stock template and changing the images and color scheme can make the site look completely unique.

You can get free templates, many of them open-source, that you can change and customize to suit your needs. There are also plenty of templates you can purchase for prices ranging from $10 up to hundreds of dollars depending on the license offered. Make sure you read the terms of use for any template you use and leave proper attributions in place if required. You can find free and royalty-free stock photography and other images online, as well as photos released under Creative Commons licenses to use in your custom website design. Make sure you familiarize yourself with the terms of each type of CC license before using any images released under them.

Use a Content Management System

Using a content management system (CMS) to manage your website will make your life much easier. There are a variety of CMSs out there, both free and paid. Drupal, Joomla, and Typo3 are just a few examples. WordPress, which is generally thought of primarily as blogging software, also makes an excellent CMS (the WordPress documentation even includes an entire section on using WordPress as a CMS).

Making changes to your website is infinitely easier when you're using a CMS. Most CMS platforms have plug-ins and widgets to extend their functionality (some have literally thousands of available plug-ins). You can find plug-ins and widgets for just about anything you could want to do with your site, though availability is dependent on which CMS you choose. This is another area where WordPress as a CMS excels; there are more than 4,000 plug-ins and widgets available, and the number is growing all the time.

Deciding on a Color Scheme

Color is a very personal decision. The color scheme you choose for your site will give people an impression of what you and your site are all about, whether you intend it to or not. Knowing the psychological effects different colors have is a good idea before you start choosing which colors you want to use. Here's a brief rundown of colors and their common associations. Additional information can be found online.

- **Black**, to some extent, has dual meanings. It can be associated with power, elegance, and formality, but can also be linked to death, evil, and mystery. The other colors you use along with black will have an effect on how it's perceived.
- **Blue** represents loyalty, trust, confidence, intelligence, and faith, making it a good choice for corporate websites.

- **Brown** has long been associated with masculine qualities and is a very stable color.
- **Gray** can be associated with sorrow, security, maturity, and dependability. It's a very practical color and sometimes considered conservative. With some added silver, gray becomes a much more active color.
- **Green** is the color of growth, harmony, and nature. It's also associated with safety and dark green is associated with money.
- **Orange** combines the qualities of both red and yellow. It's tied to joy and happiness, as well as enthusiasm, attraction, success, and determination.
- **Pink** is associated with femininity, love, romance, and friendship.
- **Purple** has the stability of blue and the energy of red and has long been associated with royalty.
- **Red** is a very emotionally intense color, associated with love, energy, danger, war, and power.
- **White** is associated with innocence, purity, goodness, and light. It generally has positive connotations and is associated with cleanliness.
- **Yellow** is associated with cheerfulness and warmth.

Consider carefully which colors you want to use for your site. Study their meanings and the impression they give. If you don't have a good idea of which colors work well together, I'd strongly recommend using pre-made color schemes. Also avoid using too many colors at once. Pick three or four coordinated colors to use as the primary colors for your site.

A Blog as the Main Focus of Your Website

Right from the beginning, you should have a blog integrated into your website. Blogs are the backbone of any social media campaign. Blogging was one of the first social media technologies to catch on and is still the primary focus of many social media sites. Mainstream media has jumped on the blogging bandwagon in recent years, with everyone from the New York Times to CNN including blogs on their websites.

Blogs have a few distinct advantages when it comes to search engine optimization (SEO). The constantly-updated content keeps search engines returning on a regular basis to look for new content, making it more likely that your content will place well in search results. This also means you don't have to wait a week or more for new content to be indexed. With just a little bit of active SEO on your part you can improve those results even more and most blogging platforms have plug-ins to help you with optimization.

Integrating With Your Social Media Profiles

Integrating your website with your profiles on the social media sites you use is a great way to get your fans more involved. There are a variety of different plug-ins and widgets you can use to pull your social media profile content onto your site. For example, there are at least a half dozen widgets to use with WordPress that will integrate your Twitter feed.

At a minimum, provide links from your website to your profiles on various social networking sites (for example, Justine Ezarik includes links to get email and RSS updates, to Fave her blog on Technorati, to follow her on Twitter, to subscribe to her on YouTube, and to watch her on Justine.tv; Robert Scoble includes links to his bio on Wikipedia, Blip.tv videos, Dopplr account, Flickr photos, FriendFeed, Kyte videos, personal Google calendar, Qik videos, Twitter account, and Upcoming.org tech event calendar). Linking to these sites allows your fans to friend or follow you and your activities, increasing their involvement in your life and their likelihood of sticking around or talking about you to others.

Photos of Yourself

A photo of yourself is imperative for establishing your online celebrity. Can you think of a single celebrity whom you can't actually picture in your head? I couldn't think of any. When I think of an actor, a musician, or anyone else who's famous, I get an image of their physical appearance in my head. I know what they look like. In a lot of cases, I also know what they sound like (but more on that later).

At a minimum, you need to have at least one high-quality photo of yourself that represents who you are (or who you want to portray yourself as). This is the photo you'll use as your avatar on every site where you have an account. It's a good idea to have this just be a headshot. It should also be a good representation of how you look, so you'll be recognizable in other photos.

Getting Professional Photos Taken

If you can afford it, have professional photos taken. A pro is going to be able to take photos that will show you in your best light. Remember, these photos will potentially be seen by thousands of people—possibly more. When someone goes to your blog, your website, or any of your social media profiles, this is the image they will see. As far as they're concerned, this is you. A good photographer will run you a few hundred dollars but it's worth it for good photos.

If you can't afford a professional photographer, find a friend who is not only proficient with a digital camera, but also with Photoshop or other photo-editing software. Here are a few pointers for getting a great shot:

- Take photos outdoors in natural light.
- Keep your primary photo simple. There shouldn't be too much going on in the foreground or the background.

- Try to pick a somewhat neutral background. Hanging a white sheet up is a good way to get a neutral background.
- Wear makeup. Even if you're a guy, some foundation to even out your skin tone is a good idea. Celebrities do this all the time. Even the president wears makeup when he's in front of the camera.
- Smile. It makes you look enthusiastic and friendly. Disregard this bit if your chosen persona is darker and moodier.

An Avatar-Friendly Primary Photo

An avatar-friendly photo has a few key traits. First, it's usually a headshot. This is because avatars are often small, sometimes no larger than sixty pixels square. Trying to fit your entire body into a photo that size will guarantee you'll be completely unrecognizable.

The composition of the photo should be simple. Make sure the image isn't "busy" and doesn't have any elements that distract from the main focus of the image—you. This is where the neutral background comes in handy.

Don't have your significant other in your primary photo. You want people to recognize you for you. And if you're doing this right, they likely won't care about your significant other as much as they care about you. Plus, the second you post a photo that doesn't include them, your fans may assume you've split up or are fighting.

Whether to include your kids or pets in your avatar is a little trickier. If you're going after pet lovers or are trying to make it as a mommy blogger, including your pet or your kid might help. Then again, there are plenty of mommy bloggers out there who don't include their kids in their avatar photos. I would suggest if you're going after pet lovers, including your pet is a good idea. There's something about seeing people with their dog/cat/lizard/snake/

tarantula/hamster that makes them more endearing to other dog/
cat/lizard/snake/tarantula/hamster owners.

Personal Information: How Much is Too Much?

This is a tough question to answer. How much personal
information *should* you share? How much are you *willing* to share?
This depends a lot on what you're looking to get out of your fame.
There are plenty of Internet famous people who keep most of
their personal lives private. There are others who share just about
everything (or at least they appear to). The key to answering this
likely lies in your reasons for becoming Internet famous.

If your goal is to gain general fame, you'll probably want
to share a lot about your life. But realize that once something
is said on the Internet and is out there, it's out there forever.
The page will be cached somewhere and anyone with a bit of
technical know-how will likely be able to dig it up in the future,
especially if it's juicy. Stories about fights, divorces, relationship
troubles, gossip, and anything else that might make you
cringe is going to be sought after once you're Internet famous.
Think through how much you're willing to share ahead of time
and then stick to your plan. Avoid posting to your blog when
you're angry or upset or under the influence (if you want to write,
that's fine, but save what you write to draft form until you're in a
better mindset).

If your goal is to push a product, service, or cause, the amount of
your personal life you put out in the open is completely up to you.
Understand that including more information about your day-to-
day life is going to make you seem more real to your fans. But just
because you choose to keep more things private doesn't mean your
fans won't care. Throw in tidbits here and there to make yourself

more human. One trick to make it seem like you're sharing your personal life without actually revealing anything too personal is to share your observations about things. Talk about things you see on your way to work, or something you saw on television, or a show you went to, or a song you heard on the radio. These are things that reveal your character to those reading or listening without actually revealing anything private.

As a general rule, the more conservative your audience, the more reserved you should be with your personal affairs. A good rule of thumb is that if you wouldn't tell something to a person you just met, you should probably give it plenty of consideration before putting it out there on the Internet. Another good rule is to ask yourself what your reaction would be if your mother/father/ grandmother/sister/future employer /minister/second-grade teacher were to read it. If you'd react negatively, you may want to reconsider talking about it online. After all, any one of those people could eventually find it and read it, especially if they catch wind of how famous you're becoming.

Information About Your Products or Services

Of course, if you're publishing a product or service, you'll want to provide information about it on your website. Putting an image of your product or you performing your service on your home page or in your side bar is a great way to raise awareness about what you're offering. In addition, you should also include at least one separate page detailing your offerings. If your product doesn't have its own website, you'll want to include more than one page. And if you're selling a service, including pricing information and extensive product details is a good idea.

Information About Your Organization, Business, Band, Etc.

Whether you're pushing a product, service, cause, or just yourself, including information about organizations and businesses you're associated with is a great way to increase your visibility. You can include this in your biography section or on a separate page. If you're pushing a cause, I would recommend dedicating a page on your website to information about that cause. Including an entire resource section is also helpful and makes it easier for your fans to educate themselves without having to leave your site.

Contact Information

You should always include a way for your fans to contact you. If you're offering a product or service for sale, including an order form or a form to request more information is a must. You might also want to provide a phone number for customer service and/or orders. Whatever you do, don't include your home phone number. Including a cell number may be an equally bad idea, though I know of at least one Internet celeb who makes his available on his website. If you goal is Internet fame, setting up a dedicated phone number (and voice mail) is the best way to go if you really want to have a phone number available. If you're not selling anything, omitting a phone number entirely is probably the best option.

You're probably wondering whether you should provide your email address or a contact form that keeps your email address private. In either case, you should set up a separate email address for handling website inquiries. This way, you can provide your private email address to friends and family while still allowing fans to contact you. If you do opt to put your email address on your website, don't make it a hyperlink. Having a linked email address will attract spammers like you wouldn't believe. They use automated programs to crawl the web finding email addresses. Formatting your address like this: your name [at] your domain

[dot] com, will prevent automated bots from finding your address. There are also plug-ins available that use JavaScript or other technologies to make your email address inaccessible to bots.

Make Sure Your Site is Linkable

Make sure that every page on your website is linkable. This means that having a website built entirely in Flash is not the best idea. The same goes for frames (does anyone even use those anymore?) and some Ajax scripts. You want your fans to be able to link to any page on your site from their blog or social media profiles. If they can't link directly to a page, they may not link at all. Adding link buttons on each page to different social media sites makes it even easier. Depending on which CMS you use, there may be a plug-in to do this automatically.

Other Things to Consider

Make sure you include photos of yourself and your products that your fans can share. If someone is writing a blog post about you, your product, or your cause, they're often going to want to include a photo. If you don't provide one, they may either include one from another source (which may or may not be flattering) or use a generic image, which doesn't help establish your brand.

Include links to online content other than just your social media accounts and profiles. You should include links to any site where you have content or that mentions you in a positive light. Devoting a separate page to this is a good idea, as it may be too much information to include in a sidebar or widget.

Make sure your site is designed in such a way that adding multimedia content is straightforward and simple. Even if you host all your photos on Flickr and your videos on YouTube, you'll want to embed them on your own site, too. Having a separate page for your multimedia content makes it easier for your fans to find your content.

What You Need to Know

- A social-media-friendly website is the starting point of any social media campaign.
- Consider hiring a professional to design your website or use a template if you don't have the skills to build it yourself from the ground up.
- You'll need at least one photo of yourself for promotional purposes. Make sure it's the best it can be.
- Integrate social media sites with your own site from the beginning.
- Make it easy for your fans and website visitors to share your content with others through their own social networks.

Blogging
Your social media backbone

If you plan on becoming Internet famous, you're going to need at least one blog. It's possible to become an Internet celebrity with little more than a blog but it's pretty close to impossible without one. Your blog is where you can engage with your fans on a regular basis and point them to your content elsewhere.

Blogging should be the backbone of any social media presence. A regularly-updated blog with useful information will keep readers coming back. And if you want to be Internet famous, you need to build a following, not just traffic.

The best and worst thing about blogging is that it's easy. That's probably why there are so many of them. The truth is, though, most blogs out there are crap. Their owners get bored with them after a week. Or they don't provide anything useful or interesting. Or they're just spam blogs filled with stolen content and pay-per-click ads.

To have a successful blog you need three things: a unique platform (this relates back to your niche and your online persona), useful content, and regular updates (whether these are once a week or multiple times a day). Combine those things with decent search engine optimization and you're already well on your way to developing a popular blog and Internet fame.

Read Other Blogs

If you want to create a popular blog, the first thing you need to do is to read other blogs. You're probably already doing this. But the next time you're reading your favorite blog, look at it with a more critical eye. Why do you read it? Does it provide useful information? Is it entertaining? Is it where you get your daily news? Think about how blogs catch your attention and why you keep coming back to them (or add them to your feed reader).

Take a look at other blogs in your niche, especially the more popular ones. What are they writing about? How often do they update? If all of your competitors are updating on a daily basis, you'll likely need to do the same. If they're updating once a week, providing more frequent updates might give you an edge. Do they get tons of comments or very few? Some niches naturally have more active comments sections than others. Are their authors engaging with the commenters they get? What are their designs like? Do they all have a similar theme or layout? If so, you may want to consider using a similar theme. When you have answers to all of these questions, it'll give you a better idea of what your competition is like and possibly how to do things better than them.

Setting Up Your Blog

The first decision to make is what platform you want to use for your blog. There are plenty of options out there. WordPress.com is where I got my own start and I now use the self-hosted version of WordPress (often referred to as WordPress.org). But there's also Movable Type, TypePad, Livejournal, Blogger/Blogspot, and

Tumblr. The platforms just listed, with the exception of Movable Type and WordPress.org, are all "hosted" blogging platforms. In other words, you don't need to do any installation or host them on your own server. WordPress.org and Movable Type are both "self-hosted" blogging platforms. That means you'll have to install the software on your own server and pay for your own hosting. There are advantages and disadvantages to consider for each option.

Hosted blogs are generally free or very low cost (TypePad has a monthly charge; other sites may charge for premium features). You also don't need much in the way of technical know-how to use them. Updates are performed automatically. And you're usually indexed in the search engines right away, since your blog's domain isn't new.

There are plenty of disadvantages with a hosted blog, though. Your site may be limited in its configuration options. Some sites charge for premium plug-ins, widgets, and other features, adding to the cost. Other sites won't allow you to do certain things at all (WordPress.com, for example, doesn't allow their blogs to have ads). You're often limited in what design options you can use. Some sites only allow you to choose from a list of predefined templates. Other sites charge for the ability to use additional templates or custom designs. And often times the amount of space provided is limited, which restricts the number of photos and files you can upload. Remember that your blog's URL will likely be something generic (yourname.blogspot.com or yourname.wordpress.com for example), though some sites let you use your own domain (often for a fee).

Self-hosted blogs give you plenty of advantages. If you add your blog to a site already indexed by search engines, your blog content will be indexed almost immediately. You also have full control over your design. If you've paid for a unique website design, you should get your designer to make a blog theme that is similar or identical for your chosen blog platform at the same time. There are free platforms available, with WordPress being my preferred option. Most newer CMS platforms have built-in blogging software, though it may not be as fully-featured as platforms built specifically for blogging. With a self-hosted blog you get your own domain name and full control over the way your site is set up and configured.

There are disadvantages to having a self-hosted blog, though. If you have little or no technical knowledge, you're probably going to have to pay someone to set your blog up for you. Some website hosts offer one-click installation of certain applications, and sometimes a blogging platform or two are included in their list of options. It's something to consider when looking for a host. When you host your own blog, you're responsible for maintenance and updates. That means you'll need to do backups of your blog on a regular basis. Cost is often the biggest deciding factor. You'll need to find a hosting company that allows you to use PHP (or whichever language your chosen blog platform uses) and at least one database. There are plenty of options out there, including some for less than $10 a month. The other cost issue is setting up your blog and maintaining it if you're not able to do those things yourself. It's probably worth it in the long run to pay someone to train you to manage the basics of your site, including database backups and basic configuration options.

Finding an Angle

This relates back to your personality, but having a unique angle for your blog is a good way to set yourself apart and get a leg up on your competition. Maybe everyone else in your niche is using a dry and academic approach. In that case you might want to use humor. If other bloggers are speaking mostly to those who already know a lot about your niche, you could offer a beginner's guide.

This ties back in with your personal brand. The way you approach your niche reflects on who you are. If you talk down to your readers, you may come across as a know-it-all. If you dumb things down too much, you may come across as condescending.

If you write in an overly-complex manner, assuming your readers know just as much as you do, you may come across as an arrogant twit. Remember that people reading your blog are likely doing so to learn something (or be entertained). Keep in mind how your readers may want information delivered to them, and what tone they're most likely to respond to.

Whatever you do, stay consistent. If your readers come to expect a certain kind of content delivered in a certain way, they'll be put off if that suddenly changes. If you do need to make changes, do so gradually. Explain why you're making the changes if it's appropriate. It makes it easier for your readers to adapt.

Start Posting

Before announcing your new blog to the world, you'll need to have some content. I try to have at least a dozen or so posts on any new blog I launch before making it public. An introductory post is a good idea, something that covers what your blog is all about. You should include a link to your regular website if it's not at the same URL as your blog.

Other post topics might include a "beginner's guide to..." on whatever your topic is about, a post listing resources for your niche, and the first of any regularly-scheduled posts. On my own blog I run a series of writing prompts, with a different prompt type each day of the week. These have been ongoing since the day the blog was started.

Keep Posting

Keep posting every day when you're starting out. Try to post at least once a day, at least five days a week. Even though many established blogs only post once or twice a week, when you're a new blog you need to build up a large volume of traffic quickly, and posting regularly is one of the best ways to do so.

The more content you put up, the better your search engine results will be. When you're starting out, finding topics to post about is fairly easy. Since you haven't posted about anything, everything is fair game. This will change after six months or a year of blogging, but we'll worry about that later.

If you're posting about your life, you'll want to give a bit more information in these beginning posts to get your readers more interested. If you're posting about a product or service, give a rundown of why it's useful and what benefits it has.

Why High-Volume Blogging Brings More Traffic

The primary reason high-volume blogging brings in more traffic is tied to search engine optimization. The more targeted content your site has, the more relevant search engines will find it. And if your site is being updated multiple times each day, search engines will crawl your site more often. Long tail traffic is mostly what you'll pick up through volume blogging, but eventually you'll start picking up more traffic for your primary keywords.

Putting up three or four posts a day (or even six or seven) on a variety of topics can increase your traffic over the course of a month or more. Increases in traffic of 30% or more are possible. Trying this strategy on one of my own blogs in the early days, I doubled my traffic after only a couple of months. Of course, as you build your traffic numbers, it becomes harder and harder to see those kinds of gains (after all, doubling your traffic from 1,000 visitors a month to 2,000 is one thing; going from 10,000 to 20,000 or 50,000 to 100,000 is completely different).

Make sure your posts are relevant. Just because you're blogging in high volume doesn't mean you can disregard quality. Mix in some longer posts with the shorter news-type posts you're writing. Posting a longer post every day or two is one way to keep people coming back. And if you highlight those longer posts in your sidebar, you're even more likely to turn casual visitors into regular readers, and from there it's not a big leap to turning them into fans.

Find Post Topics With Social News Aggregators

Posting four or more times a day is great and all, but where are you going to find that much content? After all, you don't want to put all your best post ideas when you're still only getting a handful of visitors each day.

Social news sites like Digg and Reddit are great places to harvest post ideas. Look back through newly submitted items and see what you think might be popular or what fits in your niche. Getting on the bandwagon when a topic is still fresh will reap you more benefits than blogging about something once it reaches Digg's front page. Look for niche social news sites, too.

Social bookmarking sites are another good resource for finding content, especially if your niche isn't particularly suited to breaking news. In either case, find a few good sources (at least ten so you aren't posting from the same source every day) for content and bookmark them to refer back to on a daily basis.

Keep a Notebook with Post Ideas

Keep a notebook with you at all times for writing down ideas for your blog. A voice recorder is another good option, especially if you spend a lot of time in the car or in other situations where writing in a notebook isn't a good idea. When you're feeling stuck and can't think of anything to write about, look back through your notebook for ideas. A lot of writers do this, from journalists to famous novelists. It's impossible to tell when inspiration might strike. Be prepared.

Create Some Linkbait

Linkbait has gotten a bad reputation. People often look at it as a cheap or underhanded way to get recognition and drive traffic to your site. But in reality, linkbait is simply useful content presented in a way that gets attention. There are tons of examples out there, from "The 50 best [topic] bloggers" lists to "10 ways to do [whatever]," the thing each one has in common is a presentation of useful information in a user-friendly manner.

Many linkbait posts are lists, either bulleted or numbered, or otherwise present content in small chunks. Part of this has to do with attention spans online. People want content they can scan. They don't want to spend time reading a 2,000-word essay on something. They want the basic points along with resources for finding out more.

Be Authentic

In every post you write, you should maintain a level of authenticity. Whatever your online persona, being authentic will shine through in your posts. If you don't believe what you're writing, it's unlikely anyone else will either. Passion and enthusiasm show through in the words you write.

Build Awareness

Once you have some content on your blog, it's time to get the word out. Start by announcing your blog to your circle of family, friends and colleagues. Email is the best way to do this, but keep it short and personalize the messages. Add your blog address to your signature in online forums where you participate.

Make sure you also claim your blog on Technorati, the biggest blog search engine and directory out there. Claiming your blog lets people know you're the one who owns it and raises your profile. Fans can also "favorite" your blog there and make it more popular overall.

Comment on Other Blogs

Writing useful comments on other blogs in your niche is one way to build up your profile. If you can get the first or second comment on a post, the likelihood the post's author will see what you've written and possibly check out your blog (linked from your name). Don't include a link to your site in the body of your post unless it's VERY relevant (like if you wrote a post on the same topic that provides more information or a conflicting viewpoint). Pick a dozen or so blogs to comment on regularly, and maybe another dozen or so to comment occasionally. Feel free to change these lists whenever you want if you're finding they don't ever send traffic your way.

Don't be afraid to show some personality when leaving comments on other blogs. The point is to be relevant and *interesting*. If you leave comments that others enjoy reading, they're more likely to click through to your blog. This is a great way to build up a name for yourself among another blogger's core audience, especially if you manage to regularly get the first comment (or even the second or third one) on their posts.

Link to Other Blogs

Linking to competing blogs sometimes seems like a bad idea to beginning bloggers. After all, why would you want to send your readers to your competitors? The thing is, though, that linking to other blogs makes you visible to those other bloggers. In most cases it also adds a "trackback" in their comments section (a link and small excerpt from your own post usually). While many blogs use a "no-follow" attribute on their comments (so the link doesn't improve your search engine ranking), some don't. And people viewing the comments section will see your blog included.

Don't focus just on the larger, A-list blogs in your linking efforts. Getting attention from one of the big blogs in your niche when you're just starting out is sometimes close to impossible. Focusing on medium-size blogs until your own reputation gets built up often proves more fruitful. And those medium size blogs often still get thousands of visitors each month, so their reach is not insignificant. Look for B-list, C-list, and even D-list blogs to link to at the beginning. Throwing in an occasional link to an A-lister can sometimes yield results, but don't count on it.

Holding Contests

If you're looking to get attention, holding a contest is one way to garner interest. In a lot of cases, other blogs will catch wind of the contest and post about it on their own sites. One way to get more coverage is to do it as a sort of essay contest, with entrants having to write a short post about the contest or a chosen topic and then link to it in the comments area. You can then use a random number to get your winner or choose the best one, depending on your criteria.

You'll need to offer a prize for your contest. If you sell a product or service, coming up with a prize is easy. But if you're just promoting yourself, it's a bit harder. Think about what your readers might be interested in. If you're blog has a humorous slant, maybe gag gifts are the way to go. If you're a computer blogger, maybe a gift card to a computer store is in order. The prize doesn't necessarily have to be huge. A $25 gift card, or an hour of consulting is often enough to get some interest. You can always approach companies who have products your readers might be interested in to see if they'd be willing to offer a prize. The worst they can do is say no.

Keep Building Content

Make sure you keep posting useful content as your readership grows. Set goals for yourself in terms of traffic and engagement. Maybe you'd like to have at least ten comments on every post. Or perhaps you want 10,000 visitors in a given month. Write them down somewhere and keep them in mind when you're creating content.

Don't forget multimedia content. Linking to videos on YouTube or Google Video, photos on Flickr, or podcasts on Odeo is a great way to make your blog more interactive. It also appeals to a wider audience. Some people would prefer to get their information from a video or podcast rather than reading. By providing those options sometimes, you're expanding your reach.

Optimize Your Posts

Search engine optimization is an important component in getting traffic. Using tags for your posts to highlight keywords is one way to increase each post's SEO. There are plugins available for most blogging platforms to add additional search engine optimization functionality, such as custom descriptions. Using alt tags for your images is also important and should be done for each image and each post.

Guest Post

Guest posting on other blogs in your niche is another good way to gain recognition. Approaching other bloggers to guest post isn't hard. An email with a post idea or two is the way to start. Familiarize yourself with their site and brainstorm a handful of ideas. Then email (or use their contact form) with the suggestions and a link to your own blog. Many bloggers are happy to let you guest post and will provide a link back to your blog in return, though some also pay. Make sure you include a post on your own blog with a link to the article on the other blog. Doing one guest post a week will greatly increase your visibility. One thing to keep in mind is that you don't have to have completely new content for each blog your write for. Rewriting and repackaging content is fine, just make sure each post you write has something unique.

What You Need to Know

- Blogging is a must if you want to gain Internet fame.
- Posting regularly is a great way to get traffic.
- Search engine optimization is important for getting more visitors.
- Guest posting on other blogs is a great way to increase your visibility.

Microblogging
Less time, less effort, more impact!

Microblogging, those 140-or-so-character updates perpetuated by sites like Twitter and Plurk, is one of those things people either love or despise. Very few people who are familiar with it have no opinion. It's either a giant time-waster (sometimes) or the best thing since WiFi (often). Twitter users are often credited with breaking news stories (the plane crash in the Hudson River on January 15, 2009 was first reported on Twitter. The earthquake in the UK on February 26, 2008 was also first reported on Twitter. It has also been the social media service-of-choice for at least one marriage proposal (and acceptance) and for countless break-ups and make-ups.

Many social networking platforms have integrated microblogging functionality. Facebook, LinkedIn, and MySpace all allow you to make status updates, which are really just microblog posts. But there are sites out there devoted to just microblogging.

Twitter and Plurk are the current leaders in microblogging services. Both operate under a similar 140-character update limit and both are free. Plurk shows updates ("plurks") in a graphical, timeline-like interface, while Twitter uses a reverse-chronological order format more like a standard blog for their status updates ("tweets"). Twitter currently has more users, and will likely stay ahead for awhile, though Plurk will probably grow steadily and may someday catch up. Another microblogging service worth mentioning is Jaiku, which became an open-source platform in March of 2009.

Why You Should Microblog

Microblogging is just one more tool for raising your profile. The best part about it is that it's quick. You don't have to spend hours crafting the perfect post. You can update on the fly (most microblogging platforms have mobile apps or at least a mobile site). And you can follow others both in your niche and elsewhere.

Updating your microblogging status with your blog posts and other activities you do online (and off) is a great way to connect with your fans. You can also find new followers on these services, based on the tags and keywords you use.

In addition to these basic and apparent uses for microblogging, there are other, less obvious ways to use Twitter, Plurk, Jaiku and other microblogging services. You can get feedback on an idea once you have a few updates. Asking your followers to give you their opinions on something is a great way to increase engagement and turn casual readers into fans. You can direct traffic to your sites and the sites of your friends by tweeting or plurking. Tweets from certain Twitter users with very high follower numbers have been known to cause the sites they link to to crash. Building up that kind of following is possible, but it does take time.

Using Twitter to keep up to date on what's going on in your niche is an excellent idea, too. You can follow others in your niche and related niches, as well as doing regular searches for keywords related to your niche. Joining in on conversations and trends is a great way to make yourself known to others who might never have found you through the other networks you're involved in.

How to Microblog for Maximum Results

Updating your status multiple times a day is one way of increasing followers, just as updating your blog multiple times a day is a good way to get more readers. Update whenever you post new content on any of your other sites (blog, Flickr, YouTube, et al). Other things to include in updates are funny or weird anecdotes (the 140-character limit keeps these easy for your followers to digest without taking a huge chunk of time), news stories pertinent to your niche, websites or blogs you're reading (there are browser plugins to make this one easier), or to complain or rave about something (preferably online).

Download the mobile applications for your microblogging platform(s) of choice to be able to update your status whenever you want, from wherever you are. Mobile apps also let you view the updates of those you're following, letting you stay connected all the time.

Once you've registered for an account, look for others to follow. It's likely you'll know at least a few people on the site so start with them. There are plenty of well-known personalities on Twitter and other microblogging sites, many of whom are very interesting to follow. If you're promoting a product or service, realize you're not going to be able to offer all the details in 140 characters. Creating a specialized landing page on your website to direct a link to is a good idea if there's legalese you need to include.

Make sure that once you have some followers you update regularly. Even if you do nothing to promote your account, if you update regularly you'll likely pick up new followers on a fairly regular basis. Following trends and using hashtags increases the likelihood you'll be followed more. Search whichever service you use for anyone mentioning you or your product. Monitoring what is being said about you is important for engaging with potential fans. If you see someone talking about you or your product, start following them, even if what they're saying isn't necessarily nice. Engaging with people who don't like you is just as important as engaging with those who do. Sometimes you can convert these people into fans and these people often become your biggest supporters (could be from guilt for saying nasty things about you in the past).

Following a trend applicable to your niche is a great way to get more followers, and depending on how popular the trend is, you could end up with a significant number. On Twitter, searches show up with the most recent tweets first, so you have just as much chance as anyone else of being seen. Other sites format search results in a similar manner.

Sticking to That 140-Character Limit

One-hundred forty characters can sound like plenty or nowhere near enough depending on how long-winded you normally are. If you fall into the decidedly long-winded group, you may look at that diminutive character count and wonder how you'll ever be able to broadcast any useful content in such a restrictive format. But there are a few techniques you can employ for getting the most out of your tweets or other microblog posts.

- Conciseness is key. By simply rephrasing a sentence you can often cut one or two words (sometimes more). Think of alternate ways to say things.
- Adjectives and adverbs are the enemy. Use strong verbs and more descriptive nouns instead of adjectives and adverbs. Say "I hurried" instead of "I walked quickly" or "She looked unhealthy and way too thin" to "She looked anorexic." There are almost always better alternatives to adjectives and adverbs.

- Limit your thoughts. Don't try to cram more than one thought into a single post. The point of microblogging is to provide bite-size morsels of information, not detailed dissections of topics.
- Embrace txt-spk. Abbreviate when possible. Use numerals in place of letters or words (2 instead of today, to, two or too; 4 instead of for; l8r instead of later). Remove vowels when you can (just make sure the word can't be misread for something entirely different). Leave out entire words (articles such as "a" and "the" are popular for this option). Just don't go overboard or no one older than about nineteen will be able to read what you're posting.

Things Not to Do When Microblogging

Microblogging has its own set of rules and etiquette. There are things that some microbloggers do that do little more than annoy their followers. And when you annoy your followers, it's very easy for them to stop following you. Not something you want if you're trying to build up a fanbase.

Don't send hundreds of pointless updates every day. Make sure each update you send is relevant or interesting to your followers. If your niche is cars, don't start updating about architecture. An occasional off-topic post is one thing, but if you're posting about off-topic things all the time, it becomes a distraction. Of course, if you inject a lot of your own personal life and personality into all of your online communications, this rule gets a bit looser. The key is consistency.

When you get new followers, don't thank them publicly. It seems like a good idea in the beginning when you're getting one or two new followers a day. But what happens when you start getting fifteen or forty or a hundred new followers a day? Then your public thank-yous are just annoying to all the other people following you. If you really feel like you need to thank each and every person who follows you, do so in a direct message.

Don't get caught up in your follower count. Focus on the content you're providing in your microblog posts. If you provide good, relevant content and use hashtags and other trending tools, people will find you. Make sure you post a link to your account on your website and blog to make it easier for people who already know who you are to follow you. Engaging with fans across multiple platforms keeps them involved in your digital life, making them more likely to pass along information about you to their friends or on their blog.

Keep in mind why you're microblogging. If you want to portray yourself as a drama queen, then by all means write whatever you want in your updates. But if you're trying to be taken seriously or if you're pushing a product or service, maintain a professional attitude in your updates. Avoid using crass language or posting about anything too personal. Don't post when you're angry or upset (just like you shouldn't post to your blog when you're angry or upset).

One of the biggest microblogging faux pas, however, is only posting advertisements for your products, services, or websites. These kinds of tweets are a very good way to get very few followers. Why would anyone follow someone who only sends out ads for their offerings? Where's the value in that? It's fine to send out an occasional update referring to your product, service, blog, or other self-interested content. But do so sparingly. Once a day is fine. Every other update is not. You'll know you're posting too many commercial posts when you start losing followers. Your best option, though, is to never reach that point.

Before every update you make, ask yourself if it's providing value to your followers? Is it entertaining? Interesting? Informative? Useful? If it isn't at least one of those things, it's probably not worth broadcasting to the (digital) world.

Set Yourself a Schedule

Microblogging post consistency isn't quite as important as blog post consistency. Taking a day off from Twitter usually doesn't affect your follower count in any meaningful way. Because most of your followers are following a few dozen or a few hundred other people, they don't necessarily notice if you don't post for a day or two. This makes it an easier commitment than blogging or many other online communities.

Of course, at the same time, sending a 140-character update shouldn't take you more than a minute, so if you have a mobile app available to you there's really no excuse not to. Setting a schedule for your updates is a good idea if you're serious about gaining a following on any microblogging service. Personally, I almost always post when I first get on my computer each morning. Sometimes it's a quick update about what I'm doing that day or it might be about a new post on my blog. I also try to post at least once in the late evening. I've found that late-evening posts get way more traffic than do early morning ones. Highlighting one of your blog posts at the end of the day is likely going to yield more results than posting them first thing in the morning. Posting at least a couple of times a day like this is a good way to keep yourself in front of your followers without taking up too much time.

What You Need to Know

- Twitter and Plurk are two of the most popular microblogging services in the U.S.
- Microblogging is a great way to keep your fans involved and can help you find new fans.
- Participate in trends and memes to gain more followers.
- Make sure you maintain your image and persona in your microblog updates.

Social Networking

It's not optional!

I f blogs are the backbone of any social media campaign, social networks are the central nervous system. The social
networks you participate in connect you with your fans
and with potential fans. There are social networks out there for
just about every interest and niche. And there are general-pur-
pose networks like MySpace and Facebook. MySpace is now
the most popular social network in the world, claiming more
than 250,000,000 active users. Facebook, though, is the fastest-
growing social network, roughly trippling their monthly traffic
between March of 2008 and March of 2009.

MySpace is, at this time, mostly geared toward teenagers and
musicians. If those are the demographic you're going after, then
MySpace is the place to be. Facebook, on the other hand, is populated
by a much larger range of users. According to Quantcast, in March
of 2009 Facebook's visitors were affluent (with 60% making $60,000
a year or more) and more educated (with 43% having a college
degree and another 15% having attended or completed grad
school). Many people have accounts on both sites, and depending

on who you're trying to reach, that can be an excellent idea. Just realize it will take more time to keep two accounts updated than one.

Social networks can be huge time wasters if you're not careful. You need to balance providing updates and conversing with others or you can end up spending hours on the site without getting anything useful done. While having conversations with your fans is important, doing it too much sets up unrealistic expectations on their part. If you suddenly stop conversing so much, they're left disappointed.

Using MySpace

Setting up a MySpace account is a good idea if you're looking to appeal to teenagers or musicians. While overall user numbers are high, MySpace had around 65 million visitors in March of 2009, with a total of around 3.3 billion visits (or an average of around 50 visits per user).

So how should you use MySpace once you've decided it's a good way to reach your target audience? Well, the first thing to do is set up a profile. Setting up your basic profile is free and quick. All you'll really need is an email address. Once you've got that set up, the first thing to do is customize your layout. MySpace layouts are almost infinitely customizable, though their coding does tend to be a little finicky. Even if you know CSS, you'll likely have to spend some time tweaking your layout to get it looking just right. If you don't have any CSS skills, there are literally thousands of free MySpace themes available out there, as well as hundreds of paid themes. Usually switching out the background image for these themes is relatively easy (once you've located where the image is specified), so popping in a photo of yourself or your product is something even most CSS beginners can handle (and there are tons of tutorials online for CSS in general and more specifically for customizing your MySpace profile). Spend some time getting this bit right before you start marketing yourself.

MySpace has special account types for musicians, filmmakers, and comedians. If you're any of those, you can find the special sign up screens linked from the regular sign up page. These MySpace profiles can be customized just like the regular profiles. The advantage to having a musician account is that you can upload your music as MP3 files and let people on the site listen to it for free. They can also embed your songs in their own profiles, promoting you to their own group of friends and associates. This is powerful stuff. If your song gets posted on the profile of someone with 500 or 1000 friends, that's a lot of potential fans you're reaching.

One of the biggest benefits to MySpace is their advanced search feature. You can search for people based on a variety of demographic criteria, including how close they are to a certain zip code. You can browse by religion, ethnicity, body type, marital status, sexual orientation, and more. Whoever your target audience is, it's likely you'll be able to search specifically for them using MySpace's built-in search functionality. This makes it an incredibly valuable marketing tool.

Once your page is set up, start adding friends. In all likelihood, you already know some people on MySpace. That's a good place to start. Sending friend requests is as simple as finding their profile and clicking the "add to friends" button there. I wouldn't recommend friending random people. Many people will report this as spam and that can get your account restricted or even banned. You're better off leaving your profile public (or only restricting certain parts of it) so it's easy for people to find and promoting it through your other social networking profiles, your blog(s), and your microblog(s).

There are a few useful tools within the MySpace platform for reaching out to your fans. The first one is their blogging platform. It's nowhere near as robust as a dedicated blogging platform like Blogger or WordPress, but it's fine for posting short, casual messages. When a post is published, a notification goes out to everyone on your friends list, alerting them to its presence. Some people regularly blog on MySpace and other users rarely do. It's a personal choice you'll have to make. If you already have a blog elsewhere, it might just be a waste of time.

Another useful tool is the built-in microblogging tool (status updates). MySpace allows you to not only post a short message in your status update but to also associate an emoticon (smiley face) mood indicator with each update (or in between updates). There's a huge variety of emoticons available for this and you can also create your own (by selecting a stock emoticon but then typing your own emotion to associate with it).

MySpace allows you to comment on other users' profiles. This can be very handy for getting additional people to friend you. If you leave interesting or witty comments on someone's page, their friends will likely see it and may decide to send you a friend request. Engaging with your fans in this manner makes them feel involved, too. Just don't spam a bunch of your friends with the same comment. That's a very quick way to get deleted by those friends. If you're a musician, it's somewhat easier to get away with spamming users you think might be interested in your music. Either leave a comment asking someone to check you out or send them a private message. Just don't harrass them and only message once. Pestering them is likely to get you reported for spamming.

Probably the most useful marketing tool MySpace offers, though, is its bulletin system. A bulletin goes out to every person on your friends list. Bulletins can be reposted by your friends and they can also leave comments. Bulletins can contain video, images, or text. It's a great way to get the word out to your fan base whenever you have an announcement to make.

MySpace makes a great platform for getting the word out about movies, musicians, or other things that appeal to teenagers. While some things do go viral on MySpace, it's rare and not something easy to do. Your best bet is to use MySpace to connect with fans you already have. Include a link to your MySpace profile on all of your other social networking accounts, your blog, and your website.

Using Facebook

As far as building a fan base goes, Facebook has a lot of distinct advantages over almost every other social networking site out there. Facebook was the fastest-growing mainstream social networking site out there as of March 2009, with no signs of slowing down any time soon. Its users are generally a bit older than those on MySpace (though the 18-34 age bracket still has the most users according to Quantcast), with a bit more money and more education. There's a lot of overlap between Facebook and MySpace users, but there are plenty of people on Facebook who don't use MySpace at all, or only use it rarely.

Facebook has a number of incredibly useful tools for marketing yourself. In addition to your standard user profile, you can also create pages and groups, write notes and distribute them to all of your friends, and post links, videos, and photos. Facebook apps offer yet another way to reach potential fans if you can think up an app that makes sense for your niche or your product and get enough people using it.

When you first sign up for Facebook you'll create a profile. While MySpace allows you to customize the look and layout of your profile, Facebook doesn't (other than adding tabs and boxes to your profile for sharing your activities). This means that getting up and running with Facebook takes a lot less time.

Once your profile is set up you need to decide whether you want to set up a page right away or just start with your basic profile. Profiles are limited to around 5,000 friends. Once you hit that number, you won't be able to add any more. Pages don't have this limitation. If you are offering a product or service, I would recommend setting up a page right away. The same goes if you're promoting a cause. If you're just promoting yourself, your options are a bit more open. What you might want to do, though, is to set up a page for yourself and keep your profile just for people you actually know. This way you can share more information on your profile (which you can keep somewhat private) and use your page for interacting with people you don't know. If you opt to wait to set up a page, you may want to go ahead and set all of your privacy settings to public so anyone can see your content. This may make it easier for people to decide whether to friend you or not, especially if they find you through someone else's profile.

Make sure when you're filling out the profile section you include links to your website and blog(s). You may want to include links to your microblogging profiles, too. Fill in as much of the other profile fields as you feel comfortable sharing. The more you share, the more connected to you your fans will feel.

Creating a page isn't much different than setting up your regular profile. Pages let you do many of the things you can do on profile pages, plus a few other features. Discussions are one of the best features pages offer, allowing your fans to discuss you and your products/services directly on your page. You can add photos and videos to your page just like you can on your profile, and you update your status, sending out a news item in all of your fans' feeds.

Use the boxes tab on your profile to create a resource for your fans. Adding boxes that showcase useful information and tools is a great way to keep fans coming back to your page. Think of resources that would be useful to your target audience. Make sure you announce to your network whenever you add new resources to your page.

The biggest advantage pages have over regular profiles is their ability to show you the traffic you're getting. On your standard profile, there's no telling how many people have read your news items or otherwise engaged with you. With pages, you can see statistics on how many fans are following your news feed and the demographics information for your fans. That alone should be enough to convince you to use pages instead of or at least in addition to your standard profile.

Make sure you link to your Facebook page and profile from your blog(s), website, and microblog(s). Linking from your other social networking profiles is also a good idea. Make sure all of your profiles and social media accounts are featured on your blog at the very least.

Facebook groups are another way to connect with your fans. Where your pages are likely to appeal mostly to people who already know who you are, groups often appeal to those who don't yet know you. Creating a group for your niche makes a lot of sense if you're trying to attract more fans. If your niche is fashion, set up a group to follow and discuss the latest trends (or to post fashion faux pas, depending on your online persona). If your blogs and other sites focus on cars, setting up a group for tuners would be appropriate. Don't just set up a group for yourself; set up a group that will appeal to those you're trying to reach. If you're promoting a product or service, try creating a group that will be useful to those seeking what you sell. Think about the problems your product or service solve and then set up a group for people with that problem.

Other Social Networks

There are niche social networks out there for virtually every niche and specialization possible. LinkedIn is probably the best-known, and is a social network specifically for business. With more than 38,000,000 members, it's one of the largest niche social networking sites out there. Granted, "business" is a pretty big niche.

There are a few features you should worry about on LinkedIn. The first one is your profile. While other social networking sites focus mostly on your personal life, videos, photos, and similar content, LinkedIn focuses on your professional life. According to Quantcast, LinkedIn users are older than with other social networks, with around 75% of their users over the age of 35 (only

1% are 12-17 years old). Users are also more affluent, with a full 67% making more than $60,000 each year (37% make more than $100,000 each year).

When you first sign up for a LinkedIn account, you'll have to fill out your profile. This consists of your educational background, the companies you've worked for and the positions you've held, and your websites and contact information. You can also upload an avatar photo of yourself.

LinkedIn has a couple of features you can use to market yourself and your products. The biggest of those features is groups. Groups can be created for any person, product, service, or company. Promoting your group among your contacts is the place to start, and then their contacts will be more likely to join. Another benefit to groups is that you can send any group member a personal message (as long as they haven't disabled that feature).

Creating a group is easy and consists of a single sign up form. All you have to do is upload a small and large logo, name and categorize your group, fill in some summary information, and set a contact email address. You can also include a website address in the group description, further promoting your own website to anyone who joins or sees the group.

Another great feature you can use for promoting yourself and raising your visibility is LinkedIn Answers. Answering questions other LinkedIn users have posed is a great way to make yourself known and establish yourself as an expert. Asking questions is another way to make yourself known. An intelligently-written question can have just as much impact on how someone reacts to you as an intelligently-written answer. Don't be afraid to ask questions. If you get particularly good answers, it's fine to send that person a network request. The worst they can do is deny it.

Other social networks you should consider, depending on what niche you're going after include Buzznet (buzznet.com) for music and pop-culture; DeviantART (deviantart.com) for artists; Flixster (flixster.com) for movies; Fotolog (fotolog.com) for photoblogs, mostly popular in South America; Imeem (imeem.com) for sharing music, videos, photos, and blogs; Last.fm (last.fm) for music; Authonomy (authonomy.com) for writers; and MyHeritage (myheritage.com) for family-oriented social networking. Other social networking sites are popular in other countries or regions (such as V Kontakte in Russia or Orkut in Brazil, Paraguay, India, Pakistan and Estonia). Wikipedia offers a constantly-updated list of social networking sites that's a good place to start when you're looking for appropriate sites to join (wikipedia.org/wiki/List_of_ social_networking_websites).

Be careful to keep consistent information and photos across your different profiles. When you update your photo or information on one, it's a good idea to update on all of them. If you maintain accounts across a wide range of sites, it's probably a good idea to keep a running list of them (including your username or login information for each one). Keeping a running checklist of daily updates you need to make is also a good idea if you have more than one or two sites to update. This prevents your accounts on different sites from becoming stagnant.

Things to Keep In Mind When Using Social Networks

No matter which social network(s) you decide to use, there are a few things you should keep in mind. First, stay consistent. Make sure you maintain the same persona across networks. This is easier if your online persona is very close to your real-life persona.

Another thing to keep in mind is maintaining your integrity. Don't lie or offer things you can't deliver on. Doing either will quickly make you lose your credibility among your followers, friends, and fans. If you're unsure of whether you can deliver something, make that clear or don't post about it at all. You'll save yourself a lot of headaches in the end.

Don't update too often. Keep this in mind: the longer the updates or the more personalized, the less-frequently you should post them. A status update or microblog post, because it's inherently short, is fine to do multiple times each day. Notes or bulletins should be posted less-frequently due to their length. And sending private messages should be done only if you have something important to discuss that is either personal or wouldn't be of interest to your other followers and fans.

Build up trust among your network by providing useful information and transparency. Offering hints about upcoming projects and keeping your fans in suspense is fine, but don't do things that are underhanded or deceptive. Both are tantamount to lying or not making good on promises.

Add useful information to discussions, either on your own group or page or on those of others. Don't plug your services or products on someone else's page or group (especially if they're a competitor) unless you've either cleared it with them or they've made it clear that it's okay. Even if you see others doing it, it's impolite and can end up pissing people off.

Focusing on benefiting other users in your social network dealings is another way to make you more accessible to others. Building up a positive reputation in this manner sometimes makes you the go-to person for your particular niche or specialty, and is more likely to gain you referrals from your fans and followers. In any case, being a generally nice and selfless person online often gets you further in the long run than being a pain in the neck.

What You Need To Know

- Social networking is a must if you want to become Internet famous.
- In addition to the mainstream social networks like Facebook and MySpace, there are tons of niche sites out there.

- Maintain a consistent persona and profile across networks.
- Take advantage of the built-in tools each social network offers (pages on Facebook, groups on LinkedIn) to build your popularity.
- Use updates and messaging appropriately, ie, don't spam your connections and friends.

Photo Sharing
Beyond lolcats and bad vacation pics

Most photo sharing sites started out simply as places to store and share your photos online. Now many photo sharing sites have become social networks in their own right. Flickr is the most prominent of these, boasting almost 24 million U.S. visitors in March 2009 according to Quantcast. According to Wikipedia, Flickr was home to more than 3 billion images as of November 2008. Photobucket is another very popular photo sharing site with more than 31 million visitors in March 2009 (also according to Quantcast). Photobucket offers tools for building slideshows that you can then embed into other social media sites, particularly MySpace and Facebook.

You can use photo sharing sites in multiple ways. One way is to distribute your content to other users. Posting your photos with a Creative Commons license allows other users to use your photos on their own blogs, websites, and other materials. You can choose whether you want to restrict them from modifying your work or use it for commercial purposes. Flickr has built-in tools for releasing your work under Creative Commons licenses; Photobucket does not (although you can add your own Creative Commons watermark using image editing software before you upload).

Networking Through Flickr

Flickr's biggest advantage over other photo sharing sites is its built-in social networking functions. You can set up a profile that offers information about you and your work (along with links to your photostream). You can also add other members to your profile as contacts. Make sure you include your website or blog address on your profile and upload a "buddy icon" (avatar photo). Deciding on your buddy icon might be the hardest part, as the image size is only 48 x 48 pixels. Make sure the image you use is at least somewhat distinguishable at that size. Make sure your screenname is consistent with the names you've used on other social networking sites so your fans can find you easily. Another option is to use your website address as your screenname, making it very easy for viewers to visit your site.

Browse through photos on a regular basis and add interesting users to your contacts. This is a great way to find new fans and make yourself better known in the community. Unlike a lot of other social networking sites, this is common practice on Flickr, so don't feel odd about adding random people you don't know.

Groups and photo pools are the best way to connect with other users. Joining a group associated with your niche is a great way to find others who are interested in the same thing. Contributing photos to that group's photo pool is another way to get noticed. Some groups on Flickr have millions of photos, while others may only have a few hundred. The key, though, is to find a group that fits with what you do.

You can also start your own group on Flickr. If you have a product to sell, why not create a group where people can post photos of themselves with your product? And maybe, depending on the kind of product you sell, you can post the best ones or the craziest ones on your blog (turning it into a kind of competition). If you're supporting a cause, why not set up a group for people to take photos of something they feel embodies that cause? Whatever your niche is, there's an appropriate photo pool out there.

Getting the Most Out of Flickr

Tagging is probably the most important thing you can do when uploading photos to Flickr. Using appropriate tags makes it easier for other users to find you. The kinds of information you might want to include in tags would include the subject of the photo, the location, the medium (if it's illustration or photo), the type of shot (whether it's a landscape, a candid shot, etc.), any objects in the photo, and any natural or man-made features in the photo (such as forests, lakes, buildings, etc.).

Make sure you title your photos appropriately. Using a title that is both descriptive and includes keywords is your best bet. Using the default file names for your images is a wasted opportunity. Take a few minutes to name your photos thoughtfully when you upload them to increase your chances of having them found. The title might include the name of your subject (if they're well-known) or some general words about what's in the photo.

Photo descriptions are also important. This is where you can make the image personal. You can make comments about what was happening in the photo, what your inspiration was, or things that happened immediately before or after the photo was taken. These description comments are what make the photos in your photostream unique. Your description can also include HTML, so providing a relevant link (like a blog post describing the events in the picture or something similar) is a good way to get viewers more involved.

Using relevant keywords in your titles, tags and descriptions can improve your ranking on search engines. As long as you include a link to your website in your profile, this is a great way to drive traffic to your sites. Think about search keywords when you're tagging your images or writing your descriptions. Doing so can increase the search engine optimization on your website or blog, depending on how important search engines view your photo and profile pages.

Make sure you prominently display your Flickr images on your own website, blogs, and other social networking sites. Showcasing your photos is likely to attract your readers to your photostream, where they might use one of your photos on their own website. Marketing your photos on social bookmarking and social news sites is another way to get more attention. Photos are perfect for making the front page of Digg or becoming popular on sites like Del.icio. us because they're easy for visitors to look at quickly. Photos are an excellent example of scannable content. And if you include your blog address or another relevant link in the description, that traffic going to your photo can translate to traffic to your blog.

If you are promoting your product or service through Flickr, it's fine to upload relevant product photos. And it's fine to mention benefits or features in your photo descriptions. But don't write your descriptions like ad copy. Keep your photo descriptions casual and non-aggressive. If someone feels like they're reading yet another ad, they're very likely to just stop reading.

Now, organize your own photos into collections. You can group photos based on content, date, or any other criteria you choose. Grouping your photos makes it easier for those viewing them to see similar images. As the number of photos you have uploaded increases, this becomes more important. It's easy enough for someone to browse through a hundred or so images in a single collection. Expecting them to look through an entire photostream of thousands of images is a completely different story.

Another way to draw users into your photos is to post images that are thought-provoking, controversial, or otherwise likely to stir interest. These are often the perfect candidates for submission to social news sites. Creating a gallery of images like this can draw in many more viewers. After they've looked through that image gallery, they're likely to continue on to your other galleries or to your website. Just make sure any images you post conform to Flickr's community guidelines.

The best way to get your photos seen is to make Flickr's front page or other featured pages. It's not the easiest thing to do, but if you already have a bit of a following or can manage to get your photos onto Digg or Reddit, it's possible. Commenting on other people's photos is also a good way to get them to view your images. Make sure you leave relevant comments and don't spam them or directly ask for them to check out your photos.

Other Uses for and Benefits of Flickr

Flickr is a great place to find images to use on your blog. You can search Creative Commons-licensed photos based on the type of license, tags, and keywords. In most cases, all you have to do is provide attribution for the photo.

Hosting your own photos on Flickr is a great way to save bandwidth on your own site. Of course, if you're going to be serving up a lot of images, you'll probably need to spring for a Flickr Pro account ($24.95 a year as of April of 2009). The Pro account also gives you unlimited storage of high-resolution images, an invaluable feature if you're considering whether to distribute your images for use in print media.

Flickr also hosts video files. If you're planning on uploading more than two videos, you'll need to get a Pro account. The basic free account only allows two video uploads and 100MB of photo-sharing bandwidth. The Pro account also allows you to upload HD videos.

If you're going to upload a lot of photos, you should probably download the photo upload client. This makes it easier to upload large batches of photos in less time. Other upload options include upload by email and various other third-party upload applications.

Using Photobucket

While Photobucket doesn't have the robust user community that Flickr has, it does have plenty of uses. Built-in slideshow creation is one of its most appealing uses for social-media enthusiasts. You can set up group photo albums with other users, making it great for posting images of events. Photobucket also provides album themes and scrapbook templates. These features are excellent for creating personalized photo collections that you can share on other social media sites. Photobucket also includes buttons for sharing your images on your other social media accounts, making it easier to promote your images.

The lack of community features, though, makes Photobucket less useful for gaining Internet fame than Flickr. Photobucket is excellent at what it does—storing and editing photos and creating slideshows and albums. But Flickr provides more community features and is more useful for raising your digital profile.

What to Post on Photo Sharing Sites

You don't necessarily want to upload every photo you take to your photo sharing site of choice. Uploading 10,000 photos to your account means that no one is going to take the time to look through all of them, especially if half of those photos are almost identical. Do you really need thirty photos of the oak tree in your front yard? Are seventy photos from your daughter's birthday party really necessary? Only upload photos that are relevant to what you're trying to promote. If you're promoting yourself, then go ahead and upload plenty of photos of yourself. Just make sure they're all different. Upload photos of your surroundings, too. Share photos of things you love, whether they're objects, animals, people, or places. Share photos of yourself *doing* things, rather than just posing. Candid photos make you appear a lot more approachable.

What You Need to Know

- Flickr has more social networking features than virtually any other popular photo sharing website out there.
- Optimizing your photos with tags, titles, and relevant descriptions is a very important step.
- Be careful of what images you upload. Make sure they're relevant and will be interesting to your target audience.

Video

Like TV, only better!

Video sharing is one of the most popular activities online. A huge number of the Internet-famous have become so at least in part because of sharing videos of themselves. Sometimes these videos are little more than commentary about something pertinent to their niche (though sometimes even these commentaries are hilariously done). Other times the videos might be rants about a person or company, and still others might just be something funny, embarrassing, or crazy. Businesses and individuals alike are learning how to create videos likely to go viral and spread around the Internet, sometimes garnering results they never thought possible.

Take the "Will it blend?" series of videos on YouTube. Created by the blender manufacturer Blendtec, these videos aim to answer the question, "Will it blend?" Various items are placed in the Total Blender (an iPhone, avocados, Mario Kart, Germany, a Rubik's cube, a Nike, and a Wii remote are just some of the things they've tried) and then the blender is turned on. A simple idea that has gained the Blendtec YouTube channel more than 3.4 million views and more than 181,000 subscribers (making it the 38th most subscribed channel of all time). Any product or service has the potential to be featured in videos like this. You just have to be willing to think outside the box and create videos that your target audience will find entertaining, informative, or amusing.

YouTube is the largest free video-sharing site online, with nearly 80 million U.S. visitors in March 2009 (according to Quantcast. com). Other popular video sharing sites include Metacafe (with around 13 million U.S. and 44 million global visitors in March 2009) and Revver (with around 830,000 visitors in March 2009). Revver has a slightly different business model than the other two sites and shares the advertising revenue from videos with the video creators.

If you intend to make money with your videos, uploading to Revver might be your best option. Otherwise, YouTube has the advantage with their volume of traffic. It's free to upload videos to all three of these sites.

Is Video Suitable for You?

For many, video is a great way to communicate with potential fans. Some people are naturally at home in front of the camera and speak much better than they write. While video does have disadvantages compared to text content (the main one being, videos are not as search-engine friendly), there are plenty of advantages for the right person. Emotion can be very difficult to convey in text. There are so many nuances to words and sentence structure that can change the meaning of what you're saying that it makes it difficult to convey certain meanings in text without the risk of it being misinterpreted. With video, your emotions, body language, and other visual cues let people know your exact intentions.

If you're uncomfortable in front of a video camera, then it's probably not the best medium for you. I hate being in front of the camera and avoid it at all costs (I think it stems back to having presentations recorded in class when I was in school and then played back to my classmates). Because I don't like being filmed, it's unlikely I would be very successful with any videos I made (at least, any that featured me).

What are you supposed to do, though, if you really want to make videos but just can't get past your aversion to being filmed? Practice. Start recording yourself whenever you can. Record yourself doing stupid things, mundane things, normal things, or crazy things. Then play these things back so you get used to seeing yourself on screen. Soon, you won't even notice the camera. You'll be so used to being filmed and seeing yourself through the eyes of a video camera that it won't bother you anymore.

Video can be the thing that sets you apart from your competitors. Maybe you really want to participate in a niche where there are hundreds of already-established experts. But maybe they're all providing text-based information. If you're the first one to provide videos in your niche, you're going to capture a part of the market that they can't. There are plenty of people out there who would rather watch a video than read an article or a blog post about the same subject.

Marketing Yourself on YouTube

The most effective way to get a ton of new viewers on YouTube is to make it to the home page (this is true with just about any video-sharing site). There are a variety of ways to do this. One way is to submit your video to YouTube's editorial team. If they think it's good enough, they might just bump it to the home page without any further effort on your part. It's unlikely to happen, though. Having already submitted a few videos and garnering a bit of a following give you a good head start. The more subscribers you have to your channel, the more people who will initially see your video. The next step is to get others watching your video. Make sure you share it on your blog, microblog(s), and social networking profiles. Go ahead and ask your viewers coming from those channels to rate, comment on, or favorite your video. It'll take a couple of weeks of constant marketing to have a chance of your video making it to the home page.

Even allowing a few weeks of constant promotion, there's no guarantee you'll make it to the home page. Your video has to be good enough to begin with. There are a variety of different kinds of videos that make it to the home page, but the majority of them are funny. Videos featuring animals are among the most popular, but that doesn't work for everyone. Crazy lip-synching videos are another option but again, they're not for every niche. Videos of drunk people acting stupid are also quite popular, though not the best idea if you're building a professional image. And of course, scantily-clad women are always a hit

Take the *hotforwords* YouTube channel. It features a woman named Marina Orlova, a philologist (someone who studies etymology and linguistics). She's got the 33rd most popular channel on YouTube and has been mentioned in a variety of mainstream media sources including *Wired*, Fox News, G4 Television, and *Cosmopolitan*. Most of her videos are short—running just one to two minutes—and are both humorous and overtly sexy. She has more than 400 videos uploaded, virtually all of them focusing on the origin and definition of a word (though a few videos are commentaries). Right on her YouTube channel she offers links to her website and Twitter account, making it easy for fans from YouTube to follow her elsewhere. With more than 175 million views on her videos and 190,000 channel subscribers, she's got a lot of fans she can attract to her other social media efforts.

Submitting your video to social bookmarking and social news sites is another great way to get more views. Once you've done so, make sure you ask your fans or followers to do the same. It's surprising how many people are more than happy to promote your videos if you just ask (but don't abuse the privilege).

Once you've signed up for a YouTube account and added your first video or two, start adding some friends. Look for other videos that might appeal to your niche and send friend requests to their creators. Most people will accept your friend request, though some won't (don't worry about it if they don't).

Getting Ready for Video

The first thing to think about if you're considering making online videos is your equipment. While you can film a basic video with most digital cameras or even web cams, you're going to get much better quality if you invest in a digital video camera. If you're purchasing a new video camera, you might want to spring for a model that can take HD video (price points have come down and you can find a basic HD video camera for less than US$200 now). YouTube and most other video sharing sites now support HD, so spending the extra for an HD camera means you won't have to upgrade in the immediate future. It's a good investment.

Once you have a decent video camera, you'll want to get a good tripod. This way you can set up the camera to record you without having to stack up a bunch of books on the corner of your desk or to use similar make-shift methods. It's also helpful if you're filming anything from a set position. A tripod eliminates camera shake, making your videos clearer and easier to watch.

The last bit of must-have equipment is video-editing software. There are freeware programs available with varying levels of editing control (check the resources section on InternetFamousBook.com for specifics). If you're really serious about making professional-looking videos, you may want to consider investing in high-end editing software like Final Cut Studio from Apple (currently selling for around $1300, though Final Cut Express, which has limited features, is only around $200). Professional-level video editing software gives you tons of control over how your video turns out and how it is received by others. If nothing else, you at least need editing software that lets you cut out parts of your video and splice it together in the order you want.

Of course, there are plenty of popular videos on YouTube that were shot with a cell phone and went through little or no editing.

Just remember: if you're trying to come across as professional or serious about your videos, then you should invest in some real equipment. Popular cell phone videos and similar amateur videos usually gain success because they capture something that would be difficult to capture otherwise, such as breaking news. Of course, carrying a small video camera with you at all times makes it easy to capture better-quality video on the fly.

The last thing you need to be ready for online video is a thick skin. Realize that no matter what kind of video you put up, there will be detractors who say it's "stupid," "boring," "pointless," or worse. And you'll only get more of these comments as you grow in popularity. Be prepared for it and realize that the majority of these people are just trying to stir up trouble or make you feel insecure. Ignore them. Keep doing what you're doing and don't pay them any attention. That's generally what they're looking for anyway.

Online Video Best Practices

Whether you're producing documentary-type videos or parodies, there are a few things to keep in mind. Creating good video content is only part of making a popular video. Unless your video is absolutely one-of-a-kind (like a video of a breaking news story), you need to strive to make it better than any other videos of its kind. Having a better video, both in terms of content and production quality, means your video will be more likely to get picked up by other websites and sometimes even mainstream media.

Become very familiar with your video editing software of choice. Try to use software with an active support community so if you need help figuring something out, the company's tech support line won't be your only option. Play around with the different features and settings to get an idea of what the software can do. Just remember to save a backup of the original footage before you go too crazy with it.

Remember, when it comes to special effects in video, less is usually more. Tons of different transitions, text overlays and other gimmicky effects are only going to make your finished product look like a bad wedding video. If your video has transitions, keep them standardized for each cut. Keep any text overlays simple and easy to read. Avoid text effects (like flying or dissolving in).

Watch lots of other videos in your niche to see what your competitors are doing. Look at the comments and ratings on those videos, too, to see what's working and what's not. The community watching competing videos is likely the same community you want watching your videos. Taking a little time to figure out what the members of the community like and don't like is important to long-term success.

Keep your videos short. Unless your content is really, really compelling, most people aren't going to sit through more than a few minutes. Funny videos seem to work best when they're kept to one to four minutes long. Tutorials can go a bit longer, but keeping them under ten minutes is still ideal. Short skits can go five to ten minutes without too much problem, as can discussions. Monologues are best kept to under five minutes, though the more dramatic or comedic, the longer they can run. Shorter videos are more likely to go viral, though, as people can watch and share them faster than a longer video. Think about it this way: a ten-minute video can be shared by one person once in ten minutes (assuming the person watches the entire thing); a one-minute video can be watched in one minute and then shared for the remaining nine minutes of that ten-minute time period. In ten minutes, the second video could be watched, posted to Facebook, MySpace, and Twitter, emailed to friends, favorited, ranked, and commented on. If you look at the most popular YouTube videos (with the exception of music videos from professional musicians), most of them run less than five minutes. If you really want your videos to go viral, often creating a series of videos that are all under a minute each is a better idea.

Hinting at more videos to come also encourages your viewers to subscribe to your channel.

Make sure you create compelling titles and descriptions for your videos. Tagging your content with relevant keywords is just as important with video as it is with blog posts and photos. Take some time crafting your description and title and coming up with your keywords. Check relevant competing videos to see how they're doing it. And make sure you include your website address in the description of your video to make it easier for viewers to check out your other content.

Other Ways to Get Your Video Out There

There's no reason you can't post your video to multiple video-sharing sites (just double-check the terms and conditions of each site to make sure they don't require any sort of exclusivity). You can use services like TubeMogul to distribute your video across multiple sites like YouTube, MySpace, Metacafe, and Revver (you'll still need to create a separate account with each site). The more places your video is available, the more viewers it will reach. Services like TubeMogul also give you centralized statistics across channels and sites, so you can see how many times your video has been viewed overall without having to check with each individual site.

Ask your fans and friends to share your video on their own social networking profiles if they enjoyed it. Also ask them to rate or favorite the video to make it more visible (many sites rank search results based on ratings). And ask them to post the video on their own blog or website.

If you have the money, you might want to pay bloggers to feature your videos on their sites. Consider using pay-per-post services to do this, too. Getting a few popular bloggers to post your videos, even if you have to pay them a hundred dollars or more can mean getting thousands of new viewers. You can also post on forums and use fake accounts to initiate conversations about your video. This is a black-hat technique, and if you get caught you could get banned from the forums and be ridiculed for it, but if you manage to pull it off it can be very effective. You can do the same thing with multiple YouTube accounts (or whatever site you're using). Again, this is a black-hat technique, but many of the top-rated videos are doing this to propel their content up the charts. Just don't get caught or you might end up banned.

Releasing multiple videos at one time can also prove fruitful. Many people figure releasing videos every few days is the way to go, but how many of your viewers are going to forget all about your video after four or five days? If they watch five or six of your videos all at one time, then your videos and your name are more likely to stick with them. They're also more likely to check out your website.

Another tactic you can use if you have multiple videos is to create unique tags you only use for your videos. This means your own videos will be more likely to show up in the "related videos" section on YouTube or other sites. Make sure these tags are only being used for your videos. Using just these tags means it's likely only your own videos will show up in the related content area. A really black-hat technique you can use along with this is to find popular videos (or video creators) that are doing this and then start using their unique keywords in your own videos. This means your videos will show up in the related content section on their videos. Just realize you'll likely make some enemies doing this when you get caught.

What You Need to Know

- Video is not for everyone. Don't feel like it's something you *have* to do if you want to be Internet famous. While it's helpful, it's not necessary.

- Investing in some basic equipment greatly increases the quality of the videos you can produce.
- Keep your videos short for the greatest chance at going viral.
- In some cases, black-hat techniques are necessary to make a video go viral.
- Not all videos will go viral; it's somewhat hit-or-miss.

Podcasting & Vlogging

More ways to create rabid fans

Podcasting and vlogging can be considered the children of blogging. Podcasting is akin to audio blogging, where podcasters record audio clips that are generally distributed through iTunes, Odeo, and their own blogs. Vlogs are video blogs. Some vloggers just set up a YouTube channel to host their videos and then embed them on a traditional blog. In many instances, vloggers and podcasters will incorporate traditional, text-based blog posts alongside their multimedia offerings.

Either format is great for attracting visitors to your blog who prefer taking their content in audio or visual format instead of text. If you distribute your podcasts and vlogs through iTunes, you can allow listeners and viewers to download your content to their iPods. Other vlogging and podcasting hosts often allow downloads as well. Making your content downloadable makes it easier for your fans to view or listen to your content whenever they please, and also increases the likelihood they'll watch or listen multiple times.

Vlogging and podcasting sites also allow your fans to subscribe to your feed, making it easier to keep people engaged.

Just like regular blog posts, the topics covered in vlogs and podcasts are as varied as their creators. Whether your content is humorous or serious, professional or goofy, vlogging and podcasting can be appropriate outlets. Think of podcasting as your own globally-distributed radio show and vlogging as your own talk show. You can choose to invite others to be featured in your podcasts or vlogs or just feature yourself. Interviews are popular content for vlogs and podcasts alike.

Whether you choose to do podcasts or vlogs, make sure you're comfortable conversing with your fans in either medium. If you're camera-shy, vlogging is probably not for you. And if you hate the sound of your own voice, podcasting and vlogging are both probably better left alone. If you're uncomfortable with anything you're doing, your personality and enthusiasm won't shine through and your podcast or vlog is likely to be a flop.

Before You Begin

Many podcasters and vloggers distribute their content through the podcast or vlog host of their choice. But to get more out of your multimedia content, you should either embed these files in your existing blog or set up a separate blog for them. There are a few advantages to this.

The first advantage is search-engine optimization. Video and audio content is harder to optimize for search engines to find. And depending on the setup of your hosting service, the pages where your content appears may not be optimized as well as they could be. But optimizing blog posts is much simpler. If you include transcripts alongside your content, it makes it even easier for search engines to find you.

The other big advantage is that your existing blog subscribers will also see your podcasts and vlogs. And if new subscribers to your podcasts and vlogs subscribe through your blog, they'll get your other blog updates as well.

Centralizing your content in this manner makes it easier for your fans to follow all of your activities, no matter where they're taking place. It also provides more content for your regular visitors to peruse, meaning they'll spend more time on your site and likely come back more often.

Getting Started with Podcasting

There are a number of things to consider if you're thinking about starting a podcast. A good-quality microphone is the primary piece of equipment you'll need, along with some audio recording and editing software. You can often find package deals that include a microphone appropriate for podcasting along with the software to edit your audio files. Even if your computer came with a microphone, you should probably still buy a better quality one. The microphones that come standard with many computers generally create a tinny or otherwise sub-par recording. If you're serious about podcasting, you'll want something that produces good quality recordings. There are a few free audio recording and editing software programs out there, as well as paid versions. Audacity seems to be one of the more popular free programs for podcasting and is compatible with Windows, Mac, and Linux operating systems.

Once you have your equipment ready, you may want to try a couple of test-runs. As you're familiarizing yourself with the equipment, reading a magazine article or book aloud and recording it is a good way to get started. (Just make sure you don't accidentally publish these, as it would be a copyright violation unless the book is old enough to be in the public domain.)

Podcasting, like any other good online content, needs to be planned out ahead of time. Deciding on a format and topic for your podcast is the first step. When creating online video content that viewers watch at their computers, you often want to keep your videos short to maximize the chances that viewers will share the videos. With podcasts, because they can be downloaded and listened to at your subscribers' leisure, it's okay to make longer podcasts. I would still recommend keeping them in the ten- to fifteen-minute range, but since audio content is often listened to while doing other things, attention spans aren't as important.

Decide from the start how often you'll want to offer new podcasts. Offering a new podcast daily is a big time commitment when you consider recording, editing, uploading, and promoting activities. Instead, you might consider offering new podcasts on Mondays and Thursdays, once a week, or even bi-weekly if you're also offering other content on your blog. Whatever you do, don't set an unrealistic schedule for yourself. Some podcasters have no schedule and only post a new podcast when the mood strikes them. While this is fine if you're primarily distributing your podcasts through a blog that also provides other content, if you really want to make it as a podcaster, regular updates are necessary.

Including your website address and identifying information at the beginning and end of your podcasts is a good idea, as it makes it easier for someone who downloaded your content from iTunes or another podcast hosting site to find your other content. Including this in the description information for your podcast downloads is a good idea as well. You might even think about including your website address in the title of your podcast.

If you choose to conduct interviews or long-distance round-table type discussions on your podcast, consider using Skype or another online conference-call servce. You can record your conversations and then import them into your audio editing software. Just make sure all participants know your intentions for the conversation and that the podcast will be distributed through your blog and other avenues. Check any potential legal issues in your locality before publishing podcasts that feature people other than yourself in case you need to get any release or permission forms signed.

You'll want to inject your unique personality and take on your niche in every podcast you record. Your personality and angle are what set you apart from your competitors. Creating compelling content for your podcasts, whether hilarious or controversial or instructive, makes your podcasts more likely to be shared by your listeners.

Promoting Your Podcast

There are a number of ways to promote your podcast. Your blog and social networks are the logical place to start. Put up a blog post and embed your podcast whenever you release a new one. Share that post on your microblog(s) and your social network profiles. Ask your friends and fans to share it, too.

Making it to the front page (or category front page) on the podcasting site of your choice is another great way to get more listeners. Getting to the front page or suggested content areas varies by site, but generally depends on how many views or votes you've received. This is where promoting on your existing network comes in handy. Getting enough of your regular fans and followers to view and/or rate your content (and then share it with their friends) can propel you to more visible places on your podcast host.

Distributing your podcast through multiple hosts and channels is another way to get more exposure. Making your content available through both Odeo and iTunes greatly increases your access to more listeners. Make sure you also add your podcast to the various podcast directories out there, as well. Tag your podcasts and offer keyword-rich descriptions for them to help with search-engine optimization. Providing transcripts for each podcast to provide on your blog can also be a good idea, as it makes your entire podcast accessible to search engines, instead of just the tags and description. You can post the transcript right in a blog post or provide a downloadable PDF document (don't forget to take advantage of PDF security and rights-management features if you want). Transcripts are great for people who don't want to download your content—they can still keep up by reading online.

Creating an archive page on your blog and website for all of your podcasts is a great way to make your content accessible to new listeners and fans. Providing transcripts linked to each podcast on this page is also a helpful feature for newcomers.

Getting Started with Vlogging

The equipment requirements for vlogging are the same as they are for sharing videos (covered in Chapter 9), so I won't go into a lot of depth here. You'll need a digital camcorder, preferably one capable of recording HD video, a tripod, and some video editing software. Other than that, unless you want to get into professional-quality video, there's not much else you'll need.

Spend some time familiarizing yourself with your video camera and your software. Play around with the different effects your camera and software include. Just don't use too many effects in each vlog and keep your videos consistent.

You can record your vlogs from almost anywhere, but setting up a dedicated space for your recordings may be a good idea. Of course, it depends on what kind of vlog you want to have. But a dedicated space means you can leave your equipment set up and control any outside distractions. As an alternative, consider vlogging on the go. Vlogging outside or in your car (obviously not while you're actually driving) or at the office or anywhere else you might like may add some interest to your vlog.

Be careful of what's in the background of your vlog videos. If you're vlogging about a product, make sure a competitor's product or something offensive isn't in the background. Be aware of people behind you (and what they might be doing) and ambient noise. Be doubly-aware of this when you get to the editing stage. This is where a dedicated, controlled space comes in handy. Even if you have a dedicated space, be aware of what's in the background.

Make sure it's projecting the image you want to share with the world.

Lighting is very important in creating a vlog. Use a few extra lamps if you're filming inside (draping white cloth over them will soften the light; just make sure they don't get too hot and catch on fire). If you're filming outside, be careful of any harsh shadows casting on your foreground or your subject. You want to make sure your viewers can see you or whatever you're vlogging about.

If you're vlogging about something you're filming and are not the subject of the video, consider over-dubbing your narration, especially if there's a lot of ambient noise. Using a good quality microphone once you're back at your computer makes the audio portion of your vlog much higher quality and easier to listen to.

Any online video host will work for uploading your vlog videos, though you might also consider using a host geared more toward vloggers. Blip.tv is one such host. There are a variety of benefits to using blip.tv, including compatibility with multiple formats (including Flash and iTunes formats), efforts to make shows available on demand on your television, and a distribution network that includes Apple TV and MSN Video. Odeo, the site mentioned previously as a podcast distributor, also distributes video content, so they're another possible option (especially if you're also going to podcast).

Step-By-Step Vlogging

The first thing to do is pick a specific topic within your niche for your vlog. Topics can be anything related to your niche, but try to make sure it's something you can cover in around five minutes.

I recommend recording your vlog video at least a couple of times so you have plenty of footage to work with. This is harder to do if you're recording an interview or on the go, but if it's possible you should.

Once you have your video recorded and uploaded to your computer, you'll need to edit it. Editing video is a bit more difficult than editing audio, mainly because you can see transitions in video. Don't try to edit things mid-sentence. Look for natural transitions (like when starting on a new point) and splice there if necessary. Aim for a finished video that's somewhere between four and six minutes long. Make sure you add some information about where the video came from and who produced it at the end. When you've finished editing, make sure you watch your video at least twice to make sure everything makes sense.

When your video is ready, upload it to the vlog or video host(s) of your choice. Consider using a distribution service for getting your videos up on all of the sites of your choice. Tag and title your video appropriately and write an accurate description (more on all of those topics in Chapter 9).

Once your vlog post is up on various hosts, embed it in your blog. Provide a transcript at this time, too. Writing up a transcript may require a lot of start-and-stop watching of your vlog, but is worth it for most types of videos as it makes your videos accessible to more users. Make sure your blog post is keyword rich and tagged appropriately. This makes it easier for search engines to find your content.

Promoting Your Vlog

Promoting a vlog isn't much different from promoting any other online video content. Using a distribution service like TubeMogul is a good place to start. Customizing your channels and including information about how often you'll be adding new vlogs is another important way to promote yourself. Make sure you also add yourself to vlog and blog directories.

The promotion techniques mentioned in Chapter 9 are just as applicable to vlogs as they are to other online videos. Share your vlogs across your social networking profiles and microblog account(s). Ask your fans and followers to share them, too. Releasing your vlogs under a Creative Commons license makes it easier for others to share your content. Making your videos downloadable also helps them spread. Make sure your website address is mentioned at the beginning and end of each vlog you produce so as your content is spread, new viewers can easily find you.

What You Need to Know

- Podcasting requires very little equipment to get started and the software required is available for free.
- There are many methods and services available for distributing podcasts and vlogs, some of them free.
- Producing a vlog isn't much different than producing other videos for sharing online.
- Make sure you're comfortable with being in front of the camera and don't try to force it. If you're uncomfortable, it will show.

Lifecasting
Putting it all out there

L ifecasting, the practice of sharing basically your entire life online, is the ultimate commitment when it comes to gaining Internet fame. Lifecasting is often associated with streaming video, but constant updates through microblogging, photostreams, and regular blogs posts are also components of some lifecasts. A lifecast might also include podcasts and uploaded video.

If you want to use streaming video for your lifecasting, there are a number of sites set up specifically to let you do that. The two most prominent ones are Justin.tv and UStream.tv. Both are free to use and allow you to customize your videostream page and profile. Make sure you include your website and blog addresses on your profiles.

You can also embed streaming video in your blog without using your own bandwidth. Just realize that this can be a strain on your visitors' bandwidth (so make sure they can pause or turn off the video if they choose). You might be better off embedding the video on its own page instead of in your sidebar or similar space.

If you'd rather not broadcast your entire life as a video, you can still lifecast by providing constant updates via a photostream, microblog, and social-networking accounts. Updating about your product or service is fine, but if you really want to lifecast, you should update on all aspects of your life, not just your professional life. While it's fine to leave some things off-limits, you should give the appearance of including everything (or make it clear from the outset that certain areas will not be shared).

Many people confuse lifecasting with vlogging. The main difference between the two has to do with the constant stream of information that lifecasting provides. Vlogs are often rehearsed, shot multiple times, and edited to be close to perfect. Video lifecasting, on the other hand, is unscripted and live. There are no do-overs and no retakes. Whatever you do or say is automatically broadcasted to hundreds or thousands of viewers. This makes video lifecasting a very bad idea for some people. It's also what makes lifecasting such a popular thing to watch.

Lifecasting has been around for awhile. The original lifecasters used cameras positioned around their homes, wired into their desktop computers. But as mobile broadband Internet became widely available, mobile lifecasting became possible. Justine Ezarik was one of the pioneers of lifecasting. She was the first full-time lifecaster on Justin.tv who wasn't directly associated with the company (Justin Kan, one of Justin.tv's founders, was the first to set up his lifecast). Better known as iJustine, Ezarik lifecasts virtually every aspect of her life. In addition to her lifecast, she also makes video clips available through other video sharing sites (like YouTube) and maintains blogs and microblogs.

Ezarik became well-known for a video she produced regarding her 300-page iPhone bill not long after the phones came out. The video quickly went viral and the outrage it caused was one reason behind AT&T's decision to make detailed billing optional for iPhone users. That video propelled Ezarik to the forefront of online video.

Getting Started

The first thing to do is decide how you want to lifecast. Video is not for everyone. Video is the highest-profile lifecasting format, though. Sites like Justin.tv and UStream.tv attract viewers who are specifically looking for lifecasts and video content. Promoting your lifecast through these sites is automatically going to put you in front of viewers who might be interested in what you're doing.

Getting started with video lifecasting can be very expensive, especially if you do mobile lifecasting. You'll need a constant internet connection (usually a 3G or EVDO cell phone-based connection), a webcam or digital video camera you can stream directly into your computer, a laptop, and extended-life batteries for all of your devices. If you don't have any of these things, a lifecasting setup can run you well over a thousand dollars. When purchasing new equipment, weight is a major factor. Try to find the lightest and smallest laptop you can, and a camcorder that isn't bulky or heavy. Extended-life batteries generally add more weight, so you want to start with as light a platform as you can.

Once you have the equipment, your lifecasting host will likely have instructions for how to set up your videostream. This is a relatively simple process. If you run into problems, you'll likely be able to get technical support from your host.

If video lifecasting isn't your thing, there are still some things to consider before you actually start broadcasting the minutiae of your life. Picking a few platforms to use as the basis for your lifecast is the first step. An example lifecasting setup might include one or two microblogging sites (like Twitter, Plurk, or Jaiku), a photostream (on sites like Flickr or Photobucket), a blog (the one you should have already set up by now or set up a second one on a site like Tumblr), and your social networking profiles (on sites like Facebook, MySpace, or LinkedIn). You might consider using different platforms for different parts of your life. Photostreaming might keep track of your travels. You might use Facebook or MySpace to track your personal life while LinkedIn tracks your professional life. Then you can use your blog to expand on the bits and pieces updated through your other streams and for big-picture updates. Microblogging ties it all together and provides constant updates to anyone who subscribes.

This is just one example of how a lifecast might be set up. Pick and choose platforms as you see fit. You might decide to incorporate podcasts and occasional vlogs or other videos to your cast without making the full jump to streaming video lifecasting. Limiting your lifecasting to a handful of platforms makes it easier to maintain a consistent stream of information. If you start incorporating too many different sources of information, you'll only end up running yourself ragged and possibly confusing or even alienating your fans.

Another platform you might consider using for on-the-go lifecasting is Qik, which allows you to upload live videos taken with your mobile phone. This also makes for a very inexpensive lifecasting setup, consisting of nothing more than your cell phone. Again, a 3G or EVDO connection is going to be necessary for this kind of streaming.

Lifecasting with Video

Once you have the equipment to lifecast by video, you'll probably be eager to get started. One thing you'll want to do first (and probably should have done prior to purchasing equipment) is to check with people who are regulars in your life to see if they are okay with having their lives broadcast on your channel. If your spouse or roommate or anyone else who is a constant presence in your day-to-day light objects to being featured, you may have a problem on your hands. Also realize that your workplace likely won't be okay with your lifecasting while you're on the clock.

Selective lifecasting is an option. You don't need to have your videostream live all day long. Lifecasting only when you're doing certain things (or anything interesting) is acceptable. Just realize you may not get as many viewers this way unless you stream at roughly the same time each day. If viewers know they can tune in any time to get updates, then you'll have more viewers overall. The same is true if you have a set schedule (like if you always lifecast at 5:00 every day). If you only lifecast on an irregular basis, viewers won't know when to tune in. And if they come to your channel a few times and there's nothing going on, they're unlikely to come back.

Lifecasting isn't just limited to people. It's amazing the number of video streams focusing on dogs and cats (puppies and kittens seem to be very, very popular). If your niche is focused on animals, this can be a great way to incorporate lifecasting or streaming video without having to open the doors on your own private life.

There are certain times when lifecasting just isn't practical. If you're going to the movie theater, for example. Most theaters have policies against bringing cameras into a show. The same goes for a lot of concerts. But going off the air occasionally and sporadically doesn't have the same effect on your viewers as only broadcasting occasionally. Just make sure you put up some kind of message that lets viewers know what you're up to and when you'll be back on the air.

Promoting your lifecast on your blog is a must. Set up a separate page to embed your videostream so it's not interfering with your site's load speed unless users are specifically looking at your lifecast.

Lifecasting by Other Means

As already mentioned, microblogging is perfectly suited to lifecasting. Make sure whatever microblogging service you decide to use has an application to let you make updates from your cell phone. This makes it possible to provide updates from anywhere, at any time.

As with video, you'll want to share virtually all aspects of your life. Aggregating all of your streams on your website or blog is helpful to your fans and lets them track your life across multiple platforms. Consider using FriendFeed or a similar social media aggregation service rather than integrating everything manually. This also allows your fans to follow you on the aggregation site instead of or as well as on your blog or the individual platforms you use.

Transparency is more important in lifecasting than many other social media venues. Since the point of lifecasting is to constantly update your network on what's going on in your life, if you suddenly disappear for a day or two, your fans may be upset (or worried). If you're going to unplug for a couple of days, make your network and your fans aware of it.

Another advantage to lifecasting through microblogging and social networking sites is that they're available to your fans on the go, too. Virtually every major social media site out there has a mobile version of their site.

While video lifecasting is an all-encompassing venture, once you get into the habit of posting status updates throughout your day, lifecasting through microblogs, photostreams, and status updates will only take up a few minutes of your time. Posting a status update from your cell phone can be done in a matter of seconds. Uploading a photo doesn't take much longer if you use your cell phone or a desktop application. And this type of lifestreaming is more accessible to the majority of Internet users who might not have time to watch hours of video every day but can easily keep up through multiple short updates throughout the day.

Lifecasting and Time Management

Considering that the majority of people interested in becoming Internet famous likely have busy lives to begin with, lifecasting can be too much of a commitment. If you're unwilling to completely immerse yourself in lifecasting, streaming video is probably not the way to go.

Integrating time management tools into your lifecasting platform can make your life much easier. There are a variety of productivity applications available as add-ons to various social networking and microblogging platforms. Using these to manage your life while you're updating your lifecast makes it much easier to keep organized without having to manage a bunch of extra online apps.

You might consider limiting the number of updates you provide each day over certain media. A couple dozen photo uploads is a manageable number of images for your fans to digest in a single day. Writing a couple dozen blog posts, on the other hand, is probably going to be more than what most people are willing to read in a day. Find a balance and watch to see how your fans respond. If they're asking for more, then by all means give them more. If you notice that your updates at a certain time of day or with certain content aren't getting looked at as much as your other updates, why not eliminate them? Listen to what your fans want, engage with them, and try to provide them with the content they're looking for.

What You Need to Know

- While video lifecasting is a huge commitment, there are other lifecasting alternatives that can be less of a time commitment.
- Lifecasting requires more transparency than most other efforts to become Internet famous.
- Video lifecasting requires certain equipment that can be expensive. Then again, there are other lifecasting services out there that let you just use your cell phone's built-in camera.
- Use apps you can integrate with your lifecasting platforms for managing the rest of your life.

SEO

Search engine optimization and other fun with acronyms

S earch engine optimization and marketing is the ground-work for any social media campaign. Making your website and blog easy for people to find through web searches gives you access to a much larger fan base. Marketing yourself solely through social media sites does offer a large potential audience. But search engine optimization and marketing gives you access to virtually every person online who's looking for information about your niche.

You'll notice we've mentioned both search engine *optimization* and search engine *marketing* were mentioned. What's the difference between the two? Optimization is everything you can do for free to appear high up in *organic* search engine results. Marketing applies to paid search engine listings (like Google AdWords). Those are the "sponsored results" you see above and along the side of most search engine results pages. Though search engine optimization is more valuable, but because everyone is vying for placement within the organic search results, it's more difficult to do well. Paid search ads are often used as a stop-gap measure until ranking in the top ten or twenty results can be achieved organically.

The most popular search engine is Google, followed by Yahoo! and Bing. In many cases, you can rank well in one of those search engines but poorly in the other two. You should consider which search engine you want to put the most effort toward. Most of the time, it will be Google.

In Chapter 5 we talked briefly about long tail search results. These are the keywords you'll likely be able to rank for most quickly. Long tail results are keywords people search for that might not be very popular. Many times, your website might have mentioned these terms in passing within an article without any intention to improve search engine ranking. But since competition is so low, placing very well in search engines for terms like these isn't difficult. While each individual long tail keyword or phrase might only bring you a few visitors each day or week, having hundreds of these search results can bring you more traffic, at least in the beginning, than placing on the second or third page of search results for your primary keywords. Sometimes the visitors coming through these long tail search results can bring in visitors who might not have otherwise found your site, since they might not be searching for your main keywords.

How Search Engines Work

Search engines are probably the one type of website that every Internet user uses at some point. Placing well in search engine results, while not an absolute imperative to becoming an Internet celebrity, can really give you an edge over your competitors. So how do search engines work? And why is it sometimes so difficult to place well within their results?

Search engines find websites by *crawling* the web. They use programs called *spiders* to look through every website in their index (which is virtually every website that's ever been linked to from any other website within their index, or submitted manually).

While looking over websites, they catalogue the keywords and terms that the site uses, as well as any incoming links and what the *anchor text* (the words actually contained in links) is for those incoming links. All of the information collected about each site is then stored in the search engine's index. Other information some search engines use to rank websites includes the age of the domain name (domains gain credibility as they age) and the length of time left before a domain has to be renewed (a longer renewal period is given more weight, since it's expected a domain owner who plans to be around for five or ten years is more likely to provide valuable information than a fly-by-night operation who's just looking to make a little fast cash with a one-page website featuring nothing but contextual ads).

In addition to crawling and indexing the web, search engines handle queries from end-users. They do this by searching their index for every page that contains the search term entered. If someone searches for *Internet famous*, they'll get different results than if they search for *"Internet famous"* (because with the quotation marks, the search engine is returning the exact term, while without the quotation marks, it's returning every page that includes both words, but not necessarily together). If your website contains the term *Internet famous*, it will be included within those search results. The question then becomes, where will your site show up?

Search engines rank web pages based on a number of factors. The exact formulas they use are proprietary and considered trade secrets. But some of the factors used include the number of times a key word is included on a given page (keyword density), other terms surrounding those keywords, how many incoming links the page has, where those incoming links are coming from, and what the meta tags (particularly the title and description tags) are for that page.

Keyword density is one of the most misunderstood parts of the criteria a search engine uses to determine ranking. Packing your page with keywords will not necessarily help your page rank better. Search engines specifically look for *keyword stuffing*—the intentional overuse of keywords in an effort to get better rankings. Use keywords where appropriate, but make sure your content is being written with people in mind, not search engines. What's the point of getting someone to visit your site if your content is written so poorly it borders on unreadable?

On-Site Search Engine Optimization

On-site SEO consists of techniques used on your website to help its rankings. This includes using keywords in your content, optimizing your meta tags, using tags for blog posts and similar content, properly structuring your website architecture and coding, using proper alt tags for images, and generally creating a useful and user-friendly website. The advantage to these techniques is that they're relatively easy to implement and are free, for the most part (other than paying your designer to implement them if you don't maintain your own website).

The first thing to consider is your site's design and coding. In the past, websites used tables to format their content areas, sidebars, headers, and footers. But tables have become mostly obsolete for design purposes and have been replaced with CSS (Cascading Style Sheets). One of CSS's biggest advantages is that it eliminates much of the HTML code from your site. This means when a search engine crawls your site, it sees more of your content and less extraneous information it doesn't care about. In effect, this makes your content seem more important to the search engines, because it takes up a higher percentage of your page's code. CSS has a lot of other advantages, too, but this is the primary one for SEO purposes.

Other considerations for your site's architecture include keeping all pages within three clicks of the home page. Search engine spiders don't like to crawl too deeply within your site. The more clicks a search engine needs to make to find content, the less likely it is to be found. One way to work around this is to create a site map linked from the home page that offers links to every other page on your site. This is sometimes useful for people, too, who have an idea of what they're looking for but not where it might be on your site.

To search engine spiders, certain elements within your site act as walls; some intentional, some not. Any page on your site only accessible after submitting a form will not be indexed by search engines. Pages that requires a login are also roadblocks to a spider. In most cases, though, you don't want a search engine to index these types of pages. A less-known roadblock involves any page that's only accessible through a drop-down menu. Oftentimes, you will want these pages indexed. This is one instance where a sitemap is a perfect solution to making your pages accessible to spiders. One of the biggest taboos, though, are pages that redirect before showing content. In some cases, search engines will actually ban sites using this technique, as they consider it a bait-and-switch. If you need to make a page redirect, make sure it fully loads before going to the new URL.

The meta tags of your site are also considered when a search engine is indexing and ranking your site. While the "keywords" meta tag is generally ignored by search engines, the "description" and "title" tags are not. There are a few simple things you can do with these two tags to make your site place better. The first is to make sure these tags are different on each page. On your blog, you might format your title tag like this: "Blog Post Name, Blog Title" or something similar. Your blog title should contain at least some of your primary keywords, and using the post title means each page has a different title tag. Your description can either be input manually for each page or post, or you can use a plug-in that automatically creates your description tag (often based on the first couple of sentences of the post or page). If you're using an automatic plug-in, try to use a keyword or two at the beginning of your post or page to maximize your description's effect on SEO.

Tagging your blog posts also helps with search engine optimization, especially on blog-specific search engines (such as Technorati). Formatting your blog's permalinks (the permanent URL format each post uses) to include the category name or tags can also have a positive SEO effect. Tagging adds keywords to your posts, too. While blog categories are often kept to a minimum for each post (one or two categories is generally optimal), using half a dozen or more tags is generally acceptable. Just make sure the tags you use are consistent and try to use keywords people actually search for.

Image tags are often one of the most overlooked aspects of SEO. Take the time to name your images something relevant. Use the "title" and "alt" tags, too. Enter a descriptive title for each image and a similarly descriptive alt tag. Use keywords, but keep each tag people-friendly, too. If for some reason your image doesn't load, your visitors will see the alt tag instead. This is also the text that shows up when you hover over an image. Just optimizing your images can make your site perform much better in search results, often placing you on the first page of results with little extra effort. In addition to regular search engine results, properly tagging your images also makes them show up better in image searches (such as Google Image Search).

Keep in mind that your content should always be written with readers in mind first. In many cases, writing useful, relevant content for people will automatically put you ahead of many of your competitors in the search engine results.

Off-Site Search Engine Optimization

Off-site search engine optimization consists mostly of link building. Getting other well-ranking sites to link to your content is a very powerful search engine optimization tool. There is a multitude of ways to get other sites to link to yours. Linkbait is one way (more about that in the next chapter). Building a site that's a valuable resource to those looking for information in your niche is another way.

There are directories for just about every kind of website and niche. Submit your site to any free directories you can find that are applicable to your niche. Some of these directories require a small fee to be added. These are the only kinds of paid links you should consider. Search engines generally frown upon paid links and sometimes even penalize sites for using them. But quality directories are different and search engines often consider links from them quite favorably.

One of the best ways to get incoming links is to link to other bloggers and websites. Whenever you direct traffic to another website or blog from your site, the owner of that site will see the incoming link. In all likelihood, the owner of that site will check out the source of that link and, if your content is good enough, might link to you in the future.

Keyword Research

When planning your search engine optimization efforts, keyword research should be one of your first steps. There are a few ways to go about this. Start by brainstorming a list of possible terms related to your niche and target audience. Aim to come up with a dozen or more terms. At the same time, list possible misspellings and alternate spellings for each of these terms.

Once you've got a list of keywords you should use one of the many online keyword research tools to find out how popular those keywords are. There are a variety of keyword tools available. Some just show you the popularity of keywords you've entered, while others can show you related terms and their popularity, too. An up-to-date list of keyword research tools is available on the website.

When you have a complete list of keywords for your site, including alternate spellings and popularity, spend some time checking out which sites are showing up in the search results for those keywords. Look at how the keywords are being used and in what context. These are the sites you'll be up against when it comes to ranking well in search engine results for these keywords. Pay close attention to sites that rank well in more than one search engine and take note of anything that stands out about the site. In addition to information about each individual site, make a note of how many search results each term returns. A search term that returns 10 million results may have more competition for good placement than one only returning a million results (though this isn't always true—there are plenty of other factors that influence the difficulty of search engine rankings).

Once you've analyzed the available terms, their popularity and the competition, decide which keywords and terms you want to focus on. These should be terms that are reasonably popular while being somewhat low competition. Pick four or five keywords and terms you want to focus on to start with. I'd recommend keeping a list of the keywords you want to target near your writing space, to keep them in the forefront of your thoughts when creating content for your site.

Making the Most of Your Keywords

Once you have your keywords chosen, there are a variety of different ways to use them to increase your search engine rankings. Make sure you use your keywords appropriately within your content. Don't let keyword usage make your content unreadable or otherwise challenging for your visitors.

The most valuable use of keywords, though, has to do with your titles. Incoming links are generally the most valuable part of search engine optimization. The anchor text of those incoming links has a huge impact on your site's rankings for the keywords they contain. If you can control, or at least influence, that anchor text, you're already on your way to improving your search engine rankings.

Many blogs link to articles on other blogs using the title of the blog post (or a variation thereof). By using your chosen keywords within your titles, you improve the chances that other sites will link to your site using those keywords. Since your keywords should be directly related to your blog's niche, incorporating those keywords within your post titles should be easy enough. One post that ends up going viral with a properly phrased title can propel your blog onto the first page of search engine results.

Keep an eye out for blog carnivals (blog posts hosted each week or month by a rotating list of blogs that include links to posts on other blogs covering a specific topic, good blog carnivals are a great way to expand your audience by networking with other bloggers) and other opportunities to get incoming links from popular blogs. Occasionally, blogs will run contests or group writing projects where anyone who participates gets a link from the hosting blog. In some cases, these lists become linkbait and your article might end up listed on dozens if not hundreds of other blogs. Participation in these kinds of projects is usually free and often only takes a few minutes to complete.

One way to get a variety of incoming links where you can control the anchor text is to use social news releases. Similar to press releases, social news releases are sent out to a variety of online news sources (Google News generally being considered the most noteworthy) and are often picked up by other news sites and blogs. There are a number of companies that specialize in distributing these releases for you. In many cases, news outlets will reissue the release in the exact format they received it, including any links and their original anchor text. A few successful news releases can result in dozens or hundreds of incoming links using your selected anchor text.

Other SEO Considerations

There are plenty of other details to manage when it comes to search engine optimization. Make sure you have a good website analytics program installed on your site. Google Analytics is one such program (and it's free). More analytics offerings can be found on the Internet Famous website's resources section.

Make sure your site doesn't any broken links, which obviously prevent search engines from indexing the linked pages. Text contained within JavaScript and Flash files are also inaccessible to search engines. While Flash and JavaScript elements are perfectly fine to use as part of your website design, keep your content plain text. Text contained in images is also unable to be indexed (make sure you use image alt tags in these cases).

Duplicate content can hurt your search engine results. One reason is that incoming links may be split between multiple pages, diluting the strength of those links. Also, when search engines find duplicate content, they generally select one version they deem the original or most important and ignore the others. The best way to deal with this issue is to create a 301 redirect from all the pages you don't want search engines to index and point to the one you want them to use.

Consider submitting content to article distribution sites to get incoming links with your desired anchor text. Don't submit all of your content to these sites, though, as they can sometimes show up as duplicate content and actually hurt your site rankings. Writing articles specifically for these sites might be a good idea (consider rewriting one of your more in-depth articles to a quick overview article of a few hundred words and submitting them with a link to the original version).

Should You Hire a Professional?

SEO can be overwhelming in the beginning. It's not something that can be done overnight and requires ongoing management. So should you consider hiring a professional? A lot of it depends on the time and money you have available. Good SEO consultants are not cheap; some charge hundreds of dollars an hour for their services. Every aspect of SEO can be done by someone willing to put in the time and effort. There are no special, secret techniques legitimate companies use to get you higher in the rankings. But a complete SEO strategy, at least in the beginning, might take you a couple of hours a day—hours that you might be able to better invest in other projects.

If you do decide to hire a company, there are a number of things to watch out for. Don't sign up with any company promising you first-page search results. No one can guarantee that kind of placement, at least not without using underhanded techniques that could cause you to be banned from search engines all together. Get references from any company you're considering and verify those references. Some companies will provide a fake list, knowing most people will never bother to check them.

There are advantages to doing your own SEO, too. One is that you'll have complete control over what happens with your site. You'll also be directly involved in forming relationships with other bloggers and site owners. You'll be spending more time getting to know others in your niche and what pubic opinion is of your site and your competitors' sites. When you outsource, you're relying on someone else to keep you informed. Another big advantage is the cost. If you're paying someone hundreds of dollars a month for managing your SEO, that's hundreds of dollars you can't spend on other promotional and site-building projects.

What You Need to Know

- Search engine optimization, while not technically complicated, can be time consuming.
- A complete SEO strategy consists of both on-site and off-site techniques.
- Spend time researching keywords and decide which ones to focus on.
- Monitor your successes and failures to make sure your efforts are paying off.

Linkbait
Kind of like fishing...but not

L inkbait, or content written with the express intent of generating incoming links, is often considered controversial. While some bloggers champion it as the way to build a high-traffic and successful blog, others deride it for being a second-rate and even dishonest way of getting visitors. But linkbait is a valuable type of content, one that can bring you tons of new visitors and new incoming links (improving your search engine rankings in the process).

There are a variety of different kinds of linkbait, some more appropriate for some niches than others. The main thing all good linkbait has in common is that it provides useful or entertaining content in an easy-to-digest format. Whether your linkbait is a photograph, video, slideshow, or article, there are certain things you can do to make it more likely to generate interest and become viral.

Not all content is destined to be linkbait, and not all your content should be written specifically with that end in mind. There are many kinds of content you could create in your day to day online activities that you may not even think about as being linkbait. And there are other valuable bits of content that might not result in a lot of links right away but may come to be thought of as the authority piece on a certain topic over time.

Types of Linkbait

There's a variety of types of linkbait. No matter what your niche is or which social media technologies you use, there's a linkbait format that will work for you. Whether you want to be serious and provide useful information, stir up controversy, or be entertaining, you'll be able to create something useful after just a little brainstorming.

Free Tools and Applications

Everyone loves free stuff. Creating a tool or application for those interested in your niche and giving it away for free encourages people to refer others.

Collaborative Work

Getting a number of people to work on a document together automatically means you'll have more incoming links (as each person working on it is likely to link to it). Inviting others to share their input, either by directly editing the document or leaving comments, encourages even more links. Make sure you use versioning so you can roll back unwanted modifications to the document, especially if you allow anyone to edit it.

Quizzes

People love quizzes almost as much as they love free stuff. Your quiz can be serious and teach people something about your niche, or it can be just a fun and quirky distraction. Including a button or badge for people to include on their own site (either advertising the quiz in general or showing their result) is a great way to encourage more links.

Awards

Offering up awards is a great way to get attention, since people love to win things. You can award things on a completely subjective basis or come up with some kind of complicated matrix for determining winners (whether to make that matrix public or not is up to you). Make sure you create some kind of badge for the winners to put on their website.

Contests

Just like people love to win awards, they also love to win contests. Contests can take a few different formats. You can have the winners selected randomly or have there be some kind of merit to choosing the winners. If you're holding a merit-based contest, consider opening up the voting to your site's visitors. By opening up the voting to the public, you encourage contest entrants to link to your site from their own (after all, they want their loyal fans to come vote for them).

List Posts

Creating a list, whether it's a top 10, top 23, or top 500, is almost always a hit. Consider making posts like this a series to attract even more incoming links. You could start the series with a post with a sentence about each item and then expand in follow-up posts, or you could post in detail about five or ten items in each post over the series. Consider linking out to other resources with your list, as those sites might just link back to you.

Humor

Humorous posts and videos are often a hit. Be aware that sometimes humor is hard to get across in writing. Have a few people read over your post before publishing it to make sure at least some people will get it. This is why sometimes video is a safer bet when it comes to humor—tone of voice goes a long way toward preventing your intent from being misconstrued.

Scoops

Breaking news before anyone else often ends up with other blogs and even major news sources linking to you. Getting a scoop can be tough unless you have contacts within an industry or organization related to your niche. Foster any connections you do have in hopes they might leak news to you before any official word.

Exposés

Exposés and similar content can really become hot linkbait content. Exposing someone who is well-known in your niche doing something underhanded or otherwise undesirable can bring in tons of new links. Just make sure any information you publish about other people can be verified or you risk facing issues with libel or slander.

Make Someone Else Internet Famous

There are a variety of ways to go about this, from championing someone else's content to holding a contest with a winner selected based on merit.

Design Something

This ties in a bit with giving things away, but designing something (a wallpaper, blog theme, icon set, etc.) can get you a lot of inbound links.

Interviews

Interviewing someone well-known within your niche can generate a lot of interest. If the person you're interviewing has their own blog or website, there's a good chance they'll link to the interview, bringing it to the attention of their entire audience.

Rants

For whatever reason, people love to listen to other people rant about things. The more over-the-top and melodramatic a rant is, the more people pass it along. Whether you choose to rant in text or on video, don't hold back. Just be aware that backlash might ensue, which is fine as long as you're prepared for it. Be careful of continuously repeating yourself in this kind of piece. Ranters tend to keep hammering the same points home over and over again without expanding on them or providing new information.

Attacks

Attacking someone famous—whether they're traditional famous or Internet famous—is likely to get people riled up. This kind of post can bring out the worst in people, especially the fans of whoever you're attacking. As with the expose-type post, make sure any accusations you make can be verified and supported. Another thing to remember with this kind of content is that others are likely to do the same thing to you.

Research and Data Collections

Presenting original research or collections of data can become very valuable resources for those in your niche. Research need not be complicated. Taking a survey of the features of other sites in your niche or the content they include is one example of simple research you can do. Brainstorm about the types of things people in your niche might find useful that no one else is yet providing.

Event Coverage

If you're attending an event related to your niche, consider live-blogging or taking video and posting it. Even if you don't normally lifestream, consider lifestreaming for the duration of the event.

Roundup Posts

Creating roundup posts, primarily those consisting of resources not on your own site, are a great way to get more links. Any post format where you create a lot of outgoing links is more likely to generate incoming links.

Rankings

Rankings are similar to the list post, but differ in that they use a prioritized list of things. Examples include lists of the top bloggers in a given niche or the best resources.

Resource Guides

Creating a complete guide to resources for your niche can gain tons of links. Make sure you only list the best content available and keep the guide to a reasonable size. Organize and format it in some sort of user-friendly way to make it easy for readers to find the information they're looking for. If you want to provide a really complete resource, consider making it downloadable (or create a downloadable version in addition to the one on your site).

Being Contrary

Supporting a viewpoint contrary to what the majority in your niche believe can bring you plenty of links. Be sure to link out to other blogs and site in this kind of link to gain more attention.

Solicit Reader Input

Asking for opinions is a tried and tested way to lure people in. People love to make their feelings about products, services, and anything else known to others. Whether you just post a poll (with the results available publicly) or ask for more individualized input, you're likely to get a reasonable number of incoming links. If you then respond to the suggestions you get, it's likely to result in even more links.

Satire

While this technically falls under the humor category, I felt it deserved its own listing. Entire sites (like The Onion) are built around satire, a very popular content type. Keep a running list of topics you could potentially satirize, whether images (like political cartoons), television, movies, books, or any other bit of pop culture. Industry-specific satires are often easier to promote, as there's less competition.

Be Unique or Be the First

Creating unique content or being the first in your niche to provide something or do something can get you plenty of attention. Look around at your niche to see what's missing and create it. Just make sure you do so in a reader-friendly (or viewer-friendly) way.

Taboos

Covering taboo subjects is another way to get attention. This can be one of the more controversial types of linkbait, but a lot depends on how you approach it. You can cover a taboo subject in an academic or clinical manner and strive to make it more socially acceptable to talk about (such as when discussing personal health or sex topics). You can be inflammatory (such as criticizing a religion, belief set, or subculture). Or you can be somewhere in between, offering a definite opinion without trying to intentionally piss people off.

Getting the Word Out About Your Linkbait

The best way to get attention for your linkbait is to link to other popular bloggers. Some linkbait is built entirely around this idea. Ranked lists are a great example of this and often times a list of fifty of the best bloggers in a certain niche can result in half or more of them linking to your article. Even if each of them only has 10,000 regular visitors, that can amount to 250,000 or more people seeing the link.

Other methods of promoting your linkbait include submitting to social bookmarking and social news sites. For some kinds of linkbait, such as resource guides, contests, or awards, sending out a news release might also be appropriate. Posting links from your other social networking and media profiles and accounts is also a must when trying to promote this kind of content.

Make sure you include links to allow your readers to promote your content on social bookmarking and news sites. Depending on what kind of platform you use, there are plug-ins available to place icons for the most popular ones right on the article. You might consider focusing on just one site for promoting your article, such as Digg or Twitter. There are special plug-ins and widgets to show your ranking on those sites available and to make it easier for other readers to vote or otherwise promote your content.

Other Kinds of Viral Content

Linkbait isn't the only type of content that's likely to generate lots of interest. Creating cornerstone content (or "flagship" content as it's called by Chris Garrett) is also important for building your blog's long-term readership. Cornerstone content is often presented in the form of a whitepaper, eBook, or slideshow in addition to a standard blog post or article. This type of content should be written with your reader in mind. The goal is to provide valuable information that isn't available elsewhere.

Make sure all the content you create is easy to understand for your intended audience. That doesn't necessarily mean you need to dumb things down: you just need to keep in mind what your target audience is already likely to know.

Whitepapers and eBooks are great ways to get incoming links and traffic. Releasing your ebook under a Creative Commons license makes it easy for others to redistribute your content. If you release under a "No Derivatives" license and include a page with information about your website or blog (or include the link in your header or footer), then readers of the eBook or whitepaper will be able to find your other content. Releasing information in a way that makes it easy for others to share it for you is one of the keys to making content go viral.

Using Viral Content and Linkbait to Build Your Fan Base

Linkbait and viral content are great at bringing short term visitors to your site. A successful bit of linkbait could drive thousands of visitors to your website in a very short period of time. But how do you keep them coming back and convert those one-time visitors into fans?

There are a few methods of doing this. Make sure it's easy for visitors to subscribe to your blog. Make your subscription options obvious and give readers distinct choices. Making email subscriptions available in addition to standard RSS subscriptions is one way to increase your subscriber rates.

If your viral content or linkbait isn't hosted on your site (as is the case with YouTube videos or photos hosted on Flickr), make sure your blog and/or website URLs are prominently listed in the description for the item. Also make sure the other content you have in your photostream or channel is of good quality and would be interesting to these new viewers.

Putting up some sort of gateway to access content can increase your chances of converting readers into subscribers and fans. Placing a link to your content within your RSS feed (as Chris Garrett did with his flagship content eBook) is one way to get people to stick around. Make sure that whatever content you're offering is valuable enough to get people to jump through a hoop or two to get. If the content isn't interesting enough, most people won't bother. The barriers you erect to access the content should grow increasingly more difficult as the importance of the information increases.

Create a widget, badge, or button related to your content to make it easy for other site owners and bloggers to promote you and your site. Have a variety of sizes available to make it easy for others to use. Involving your readers in promoting your content turns them into evangelists for you. Making it easy and rewarding for people to promote you makes them more likely to continue promoting you in the future. Make sure you also send a quick "thank you" email to anyone who sends you a large amount of traffic. It's a nice touch that's likely to set you apart from others in your niche.

Giving Content Away

Giving content away can be another excellent way to get your name out there as an expert in your field. And by giving content away, I'm not just talking about posting it on your blog for free. There's a growing movement online that gives away content either under Creative Commons licenses or even by completely releasing the copyright.

Creative Commons

Creative Commons is an organization that offers licenses for releasing content in an effort to make it easier to distribute and build upon the content of others. There are a number of license options, from the least restrictive Attribution license (which just requires that you credit the original creator) to most most restrictive Attribution Non-Commercial No Derivatives license (which means you have to give credit, you can't change anything, and you can't sell the content or otherwise use it commercially).

These licenses can be used for videos, audio content, photos, articles, and pretty much anything else that could be copyrighted.

The licenses are free to use and can be used by anyone in the world. It's not a replacement for copyright. Your work still remains your property and you retain the copyright to it. But the Creative Commons licenses allow others to use your work and redistribute it, either in it's original form or modified.

The biggest advantage to licensing your work like this is that it's more likely to be used by others and credited back to you. This gets your name out there as an expert in your field. Letting others use your photos, articles, videos, and other content builds a sense of respect among your peers. It paints you as a generous person who is willing to share their knowledge and contribute to the community that exists within your niche without regard to personal gain.

Of course, there are disadvantages to Creative Commons. First, you have no control over who uses your content. Your biggest competitor could use it. Or it could show up on spam blogs with your name attached. And nothing says the people who use your content have to provide anything more than a byline. If you have a common name, this might not necessarily work in your favor, especially if you're relatively unknown to start. Another disadvantage is that if you use a license that allows for derivatives, you have no control over what kinds of derivative works can be made. Your photos could be used to promote something you're against (with your name then attached). Your articles could be changed and made inaccurate while still having your name attached.

Creative Commons can be a trade off. It does get your name out there more, but sometimes in ways you wouldn't necessarily want. My best recommendation is to try it out and see how it works for you. Success is going to vary depending on the content you create and the niche you're working in. In most cases, Creative Commons seems to have many more positive results than negative ones.

Releasing Copyright

Releasing copyright is a much more extreme way of giving your content away. In this case, you release all rights to your work. You're allowing others to take your work, do with it as they please, with no requirement to credit you. They can make money off of it, put their own name on it and claim it as their own (though it's not possible for them to then copyright it, especially if no substantial changes have been made), or they can tear it apart and rebuild it into something better (or worse) without crediting you for the original idea.

I'm sure at this point, most of you are wondering why anyone would ever willingly do something like that. It's not yet a widespread practice, so finding people who have much experience in this is tough. But there is at least one incredibly popular blog, Zen Habits (http://zenhabits.net), that has done just that. Leo Babauta, the author of the Zen Habits blog and *The Power of Less* book, released the copyright to all of the content on the blog and for his *Zen Habits* ebook back in January 2008. Leo's reasoning behind uncopyrighting his content is sound. Here it is, in his own words:

> "I'm not a big fan of copyright laws anyway, especially as they're being applied these days by corporations, used to crack down on the little guys so they can continue their large profits.
>
> "Copyrights are often touted as protecting the artist, but in most cases the artist gets very little while the corporations make most of the money. I'm trying this experiment to see whether releasing copyright really hurts the creator of the content.
>
> "I think, in most cases, the protectionism that is touted by 'anti-piracy' campaigns and lawsuits and lobbying actually hurts the artist. Limiting distribution to protect profits isn't a good thing.

"The lack of copyright, and blatant copying by other artists and even businesses, never hurt Leonardo da Vinci when it comes to images such as the Mona Lisa, the Last Supper, or the Vitruvian Man. It's never hurt Shakespeare. I doubt that it's ever really hurt any artist (although I might just be ignorant here).

"And while I'm no da Vinci or Shakespeare, I can't help but wonder whether copyright hurts me or helps me. If someone feels like sharing my content on their blog, or in any other form for that matter, that seems like a good thing for me. If someone wanted to share my ebook with 100 friends, I don't see how that hurts me. My work is being spread to many more people than I could do myself. That's a plus, as I see it.

"And if someone wants to take my work and improve upon it, as artists have been doing for centuries, I think that's a wonderful thing. If they can take my favorite posts and make something funny or inspiring or thought-provoking or even sad … I say more power to them. The creative community only benefits from derivations and inspirations.

"This isn't a new concept, of course, and I'm freely ripping ideas off here. Which is kinda the point."

For anyone interested in this concept, I'd highly recommend reading the rest of his post (http://zenhabits.net/2008/01/open-source-blogging-feel-free-to-steal-my-content/) on the concept, including his response to common arguments against uncopyrighting. When asked whether uncopyrighting has had any unintended effects, Leo responded, "One thing that has amazed me is the overwhelming positive response I've received as a response to my uncopyright. I've had hundreds and hundreds of commenters, emails, and blog posts lauding my move and calling me 'generous'. This isn't something I intended or hoped for, but it's very gratifying and very encouraging." Leo's blog remains in the top 100 blogs online; pretty compelling evidence that releasing copyright doesn't have any major negative consequences.

Here's a bit more on what Leo had to say about the effects of uncopyrighting his work: "It's hard to separate the effects of uncopyrighting from my other efforts to grow my blog and spread my brand as a writer, but there's no doubt in my mind that uncopyrighting has helped in a large way in reaching new audiences and increasing my subscriber count and ebook sales. My subscriber number has more than doubled since I released copyright, and ebook sales are greater than ever.

"I've also reached readers in new ways -- ways that would never have been possible before my uncopyright. For example, teachers have used my articles in their classrooms, organizations have used my writing in their newsletters (both print and email), I've been published in several magazines due to uncopyright, and I've been in print books as well. That's really amazing to me."

Some people, when presented with the idea of releasing the copyright to their work, are afraid that their work will never be credited to them and they'll never see any benefit from what they've created. While this is possible, it doesn't seem to be the norm. More from Leo: "...I rarely see uncredited uses of my work. Perhaps that's just because I don't scour the net anymore, as I did when this used to bother me. But for the most part, people are very generous in crediting me for any writing they've used or ideas they quote. Uncredited uses of my work is not a problem in the slightest."

Again, this seems like a viable option to try, at the very least. You could always start by offering an ebook or whitepaper with no copyright. Ask those who redistribute it to include a link back to your website and credit, but don't require it. See what your response is. It could be fantastic, or it could be limited. You may find that 90% of those who share it link back to you and that you receive a huge increase in traffic from it. Or you might have the opposite effect and find that no one credits you and you see no increase in traffic (which seems unlikely based on the experience of others). The main thing is to offer content that's compelling and that others would want to share.

Remember, any time you're encouraging others to distribute your content for you, and any time you make it easier for them to do so, you're likely to see some benefit from it in terms of name recognition and increased interest. And those are the keys to becoming Internet famous!

What You Need to Know

- There are more than twenty different kinds of linkbait.
- Whitepapers, eBooks, and other cornerstone content can help build long-term authority.
- Controversy can be a great way to get incoming links and attention, but isn't necessary to building a successful linkbait piece.
- Make sure all of your content is either useful or entertaining (or both).

Information
Pretty much the whole
point of the web

Information aggregation has largely become the lifeblood of the web. Sites like Wikipedia, Squidoo, and all the niche wiki sites out there are visited by hundreds of millions of people each month. Wikipedia is one of the most popular sites online, with somewhere around 75 million US visitors during March 2009 according to Quantcast.

The thing all of these sites have in common is that they're built by users. Wikipedia is editable by anyone and employs a peer-review system for checking references and verifying information. Sites like Squidoo contain pages built by individual users on just about any topic imaginable. Other sites such as Mahalo, Hubpages, and even how-to sites like WikiHow and eHow contain similar user-generated content.

There are a few different ways you can use pages and sites like these to promote yourself. Creating a page about yourself is the most obvious way. But sites like Wikipedia won't allow you to have a page about yourself until you're well-known. Squidoo, on the other hand, has a special sub-site called SquidWho dedicated to building pages about all sorts of people, famous or not. You can build your own page there or build pages about others.

A more common way to build your notoriety on these types of sites, though, is to build or contribute to pages related to your niche. Building a page on Squidoo or Hubpages is easy enough and only requires a bit of time and a free account. Contributing to wikis takes a bit more finesse to get the best results, as you have to be a bit more roundabout in how you push yourself, your blog, and your other online activities.

Working with Wikis

The word "wiki" refers to the architecture a site is built on. Wikis are generally editable by anyone who visits (though sometimes they're only editable by those with an account or those who have been invited by the wiki creator). They also usually use a specific type of markup for formatting their pages. Wikipedia, the user-edited encyclopedia, is the most popular wiki site on the web. But there are tons of others, mostly topical sites that focus on one niche or another. There are also sites where you can create your own wiki on any topic you want.

Wikipedia has one of the most active user communities of any wiki around. Literally within minutes of suggesting a change to a page, others will be jumping on board either to back you up or to shut you down. Page content shifts continuously as users edit and refine the information. You have to be wary of some articles on Wikipedia, though, as all the content isn't necessarily accurate. There have been reports almost from the site's beginnings of people going in and editing their own pages or the pages of their company so they're reflected in a more positive light. One notable example includes Stephen Colbert editing the African elephant page to increase their population numbers, hoping to get them removed from the endangered species list.

One way of using Wikipedia for increasing your profile is to find pages where your own content can be incorporated as a source for an article's content. If you've interviewed someone who has a Wikipedia page, gotten the scoop on a news story, or done some original research, editing the article to use your content in the footnotes for the article can drive traffic your way.

Consider creating a topical wiki for your niche if there isn't one already. You can install wiki software on your own web server or have your wiki hosted on one of numerous wiki farms out there (PBWiki and WetPaint are two of the most popular). Mediawiki, the software Wikipedia is built on, is open source and available for free, but there are plenty of other wiki platforms available out there.

Niche wikis, because of their collaborative nature, make great linkbait. Get the word out about your wiki through your other social networking profiles and social bookmarking and news sites. Specifically asking other leaders in your niche to contribute to your wiki can also be a great way to get attention and incoming links. Plus, people always like being recognized as leaders in their field, making them more likely to pass the word along to their readers.

If you opt to start your own niche wiki, make sure you populate it with some sample content first. Also set up guidelines and a "user guide" for those who want to contribute. You'll need to moderate content, since spammers often love to use unmoderated wikis to push their own agenda.

Your niche may already have a wiki, though. If so, become a contributor. You can use the same methods mentioned for Wikipedia on niche wikis (just double check the wiki's guidelines first). Listing your content as a resource establishes you as an expert within your niche and improves your credibility.

Squidoo, Hubpages, and Similar Sites

The big advantage sites like Squidoo and Hubpages have over wikis is that you have full control over the content you create. The value of this should not be underestimated. When you make a contribution to a wiki, there's a good chance someone will change or even delete those contributions entirely. With this type of page, "lens" (as they're called on Squidoo) or "hub" (as they're called on Hubpages), you have complete control over your content.

There are a number of ways to use these kinds of sites. The most obvious way is to create a lens about yourself. If you're pushing a product or service, build a page about it. Make sure to build a page about your cause if that's what you're looking to become famous for. After you've built these basic lenses, start building others about your niche. Make sure you link to your own content heavily within these pages, but also link out to other valuable content.

These types of pages can build authority by getting links from other websites (and other pages or lenses). As their authority and ranking grows, the links they contain to your other content will increase in value. And as with hosted blogs, these pages benefit from being located at an established domain and are indexed by search engines almost immediately.

One thing to remember when it comes to building pages on these kinds of sites is that the tighter your niche, the better your page will do. Part of this has to do with search engine optimization. You're better off linking in the top five or ten results for a very specific search term than ranking 100 or even 50 in a very broad search. One reason is that the person searching for something very specific is likely going to spend more time looking through the content you're providing (including those outgoing links to your website and blog). Another reason is that the person looking for something specific will actually find your site, since you'll be on the first page of search results. If you're buried five or ten pages in, only a very small portion of people searching will make it that far.

Your goal in all this is to create *quality* traffic, not just quantity. You want to connect with people who are likely to become fans. You want your readers to connect with you on a level that keeps them coming back for more and has them telling their friends about you. That kind of relationship building is done through providing something that no one else is providing, either in its delivery or in the content itself.

Building Your Pages

Don't mistake the simple setup and standard format to mean you won't need excellent content for these pages. While there are slightly different standards depending on which site you're using, there are some basic guidelines to follow when creating your content.

The information you're providing has to be valuable to your target audience. Check around to see if there are competing pages or lenses and offer up something they don't. Keep in mind what kinds of things you would want to know if you were new to a subject.

Make sure you use effective keywords and tags in your pages. The keyword research you did earlier for your search engine optimization plan will come in handy here. Take advantage of titles and subheadings and make sure you use keywords there. If the site you're building a page on will allow you to choose your own URL (most of them do), take advantage of it by using your keywords there, too. Search engines place some weight in the website address for a page when calculating its ranking.

When creating your content, make sure you have enough different content sections within the page. On Squidoo, these are called modules; on Hubpages they're called capsules. Each of these sections can contain a different kind of content. You can add videos, photos, affiliate links, and a variety of other content types in addition to standard text.

Use images or other multimedia content within your lens. Try to make sure there's at least one photo or video in each section, unless that section contains affiliate links or a list of some kind. Name your images and provide alternate text that will assist in your page's search engine optimization.

Include plenty of outgoing links from your pages and be sure you incorporate any of your other content (videos, photos, podcasts or other multimedia content) that fits with the topic of the lens or hub.

Also make your pages interactive. Many of these sites include modules for incorporating a poll, ranking, or debate on your page. Getting your visitors involved in the content of your pages makes them more likely to remember your page, to bookmark it for later reference, and to tell their friends about it or link to it from their own blog.

Promoting Your Pages

In addition to your individual pages, make sure you spend some time on your profile. Upload an avatar or profile photo (the same one you use on all your other social media profiles). Create a short bio with information about who you are and don't forget to add links to your blog, website, and any other sites allowed (such as your Twitter profile or YouTube channel).

Creating a widget for your blog that lists your lenses or hubs is one way to promote them. Consider making the widget available for others to place on their blogs or sites. And be sure to place your widget on your social networking profiles.

Each time you create or make major changes to a lens, you should announce it on your blog and on your social media profiles and accounts.

Network with others who participate on the site you're using. Almost all of these kinds of sites have member groups you can join. Join groups related to your niche and network with other members.

Post useful comments on related pages. If you post something interesting or otherwise helpful, it's likely the person who maintains that page will check out your pages in return. That increases the chances they'll include your page or even your blog as a resource in new pages they create. You might consider doing the same thing for anyone who comments on your pages.

What You Need to Know

- There are special techniques you can use to promote yourself on wikis.
- Sites like Hubpages and Squidoo are great places to promote yourself.
- Put time and effort into pages you build just as you would on your own blog or website.
- SEO is just as important for these kinds of pages as it is on your blog or website.

Social News & Bookmarking
Staying on top of what's happening online

S ocial news and social bookmarking sites are two of the best ways to promote your content and find new readers. While search engines help you find people who were already looking for what you offer, social news and bookmarking sites can connect you with people who didn't even know your niche existed. And so, if you do your job right, you can connect with people who might not otherwise have ever become your fans.

There is a huge variety of social news sites out there, ranging from general news sites that cover just about anything to niche sites focusing on one specific type of content. Depending on your niche, you may be able to employ both types of sites. Digg and Reddit are two of the largest general social news sites. Both work on the premise of letting users submit and vote on material. Generally speaking, material with the most votes ends up on the front page of the site (though the algorithms these sites use are more complicated than that).

Social bookmarking sites, on the other hand, work much like a social network. On most sites, you can friend or follow other users and see the sites they share, recommend, and bookmark. This is a great way to connect with others who are interested in your niche.

Making it to the front page of a niche social news site can draw hundreds of new visitors to your site. One of the good things these visitors bring is that they're very likely to be active in your niche; after all, they were referred by a site focused on your niche. Because of their interest, it's likely a large percentage of them will stick around. Of course, making it to the front page of a major social news site like Digg or Reddit can drive thousands of new visitors to your site. The quality of this traffic is generally not as high as the quality of visitors from niche sites, but you're still likely to pick up a fair number of new subscribers and regular readers.

One of the biggest advantages to attracting visitors from these sites and converting them to subscribers and regular readers is that these visitors are already users of the social news and bookmarking sites you're targeting. As you gain more and more returning visitors from these sites, your content is more likely to be voted up in the future. This is how some sites manage to get almost all of their major content to the front page or popular section.

Getting Started with Social News Sites

Social news sites can be daunting at first glance. On some of the larger sites, such as Digg, the items that make the front page might have anywhere from a few dozen to a few hundred votes. When you have very few followers on your blog, getting those kinds of numbers might seem impossible. But on smaller niche-specific sites, it might only take a dozen or so votes to make the front page.

Once you've signed up for an account, you may want to spend some time exploring the site and its dynamics before diving in and submitting your content. Figure out which users seem to be the most popular and who seems to submit the most content to make it to the popular section. Each site generally has their own set of "power users" who have more influence over what becomes popular, either just by influencing other users or through the site's algorithm.

Using your social news site of choice on a regular basis is one key to success. Submit content on a regular basis to gain more traction. Make sure you vote for other content, too, or you'll end up looking like a spammer more than a participant. And spamming sites like these does little to improve your popularity.

Make sure you research which sites are appropriate for promoting your content. Look over the kinds of topics that are making it to the front page or popular area of the site. What kind of content are they offering? What format are they presenting it in? Are most of the popular posts lists? Videos? Slideshows? Longer articles? Shorter articles? Take a survey of what seems to be most popular. Keep an eye on the site for a week or more to see if there are trends.

Once you have some idea of what kinds of content are suitable for the site, start submitting some content. At first, you may want to experiment with what to submit and when to submit it. Different times of day may be more or less active than others. You may not want to submit your best content at first, before you've built up a few submissions. You might also try submitting other people's content as a test.

As you get the hang of the site, make sure you keep submitting content on a regular basis. At the same time, comment on the submissions of others to make yourself more visible. Submitting or commenting on a handful of items each day is a bit of a time commitment but should be your goal if you really want to get the most out of social news sites.

Timing is one of the most important parts of reaching the popular section of a social news site. A post that gets 50 votes in a matter of minutes is well on its way to getting to the front page of most social news sites. A post that gets 200 visits over the course of a week isn't likely to make it. Posting at the times of day when other members are active, as well as at times when your blog is getting a lot of traffic, increases your likelihood of becoming popular. Almost every social news site has an "up and coming" or "newly posted" section where members scan for new content to vote up or down. Being on this page at peak times is a great way to get noticed.

Making the Most of Social Bookmarking

The most popular social bookmarking site is Delicious. Social bookmarking sites like this generally have "popular" pages similar to the ones on social news sites. The main difference between the two comes down to their purpose. News sites aim to promote timely content to a large audience. Bookmarking sites work more like the bookmarks you can save in your browser. Their aim is to save very useful and relevant content for later reference.

Research your social bookmarking site(s) of choice just as you did the social news sites. Figure out who the power users are and see if your content fits with the types of things they regularly submit. Figure out which types of content do well on the site and what the best time of day is to submit things. On Delicious, for example, the most popular types of articles (based on popular tags) seem to be how-to guides, reference manuals, tools, tips, inspiration, and freebies. This type of research can generally be done in a few minutes, just by looking at the types of things on the popular pages and the site's tag cloud (if there is one).

Getting your content noticed on these sites has a lot to do with connecting with other users. Find users who are promoting similar content and friend or follow them. Building up a large network of friends over a long period of time makes it more likely the content you submit will become popular. Make sure you don't just submit your own content, though. Submit anything you find useful, including your own content.

Strategies for Both Kinds of Sites

There are certain strategies for getting your content seen on both social news and social bookmarking sites. One method is to ask your regular readers to vote for your content on these sites. Depending on the CMS or blogging platform you're using, there should be a plugin or widget to make submission easier. Evangelizing your readers in this manner can go a long way toward making your content popular. Even if you only have a few hundred regular readers, if you can get a large percentage of them to submit or vote for your content, you can make the front page or popular page of most of these sites with those kinds of number. Niche sites, on average, take even fewer votes.

Don't be afraid to ask your regular readers and those you connect with on social networking sites to vote for your content. If you have a microblog, send out a link to the page on the social news site of your choice and ask people to vote instead of linking directly to the article. Getting those who are already your fans to vote up your content is a great strategy when you're starting out and can get you more attention for established users of these social media sites.

Make sure you use these sites on a regular basis. Daily is best, but weekly is pretty much the minimum for developing an effective strategy. Voting up the content of others in addition to your own makes it more likely you'll be accepted as a member of the community. And being accepted goes a long way toward consistently placing your content in the popular sections.

Building up a profile as an influencer (who's submissions regularly make the front page or popular sections) on these sites and gaining a large number of friends is the next step. One way is to friend people whose content you vote for. There are a few advantages to having a high-powered profile. One is the ability to promote your own content. The other is to be able to promote the content of other bloggers. That can be a great way to connect with other site owners and possibly get them to promote your content, either on their site or through the social news and bookmarking sites they actively use.

Again, the most important part of using these sites to your best advantage is to become an active member of the community. Use the site as often as you can. Write ten or fifteen minutes a day (or more, if you have the time) into your schedule specifically for participating. Focus on two or three sites to start so you don't spread yourself too thin. If you try to become popular on ten or fifteen sites at once, it's likely you won't succeed on any of them.

In addition to following the linkbait principles in Chapter 13, make sure your headline is crafted to intrigue. Headlines that offer some concrete information about your post and promise something to those who read it are most effective. Headlines such as "13 Surefire Ways to Get Your Content to the Front Page of Digg" or "The Top 10 Methods for Doubling Your Blog Traffic" are more likely to get attention than "Make Your Content More Popular" or "Get More Blog Visitors." Spend some time on your title to make it as eye-catching as possible.

Types of Content Best Suited for These Sites

There are specific types of content best suited for social news sites and social bookmarking sites. While there is some overlap, some types are more suited to one or the other.

The popular content on social news sites tends to be timely. While resource pages and tutorials also regularly make it to the front page of Digg or Reddit, they're often tied into some news announcement or other current events. Other common content types on social news site are the wacky or off beat.

Social bookmarking sites, on the other hand, are often populated more with resources you might want to consult at a later date. Tutorials, inspiration, how-to articles, and reference guides all have a good chance of gaining popularity. With really useful content, you're more likely to have other users also bookmark your submissions.

Spend time perfecting content you hope will get to the front pages of these sites. If your content isn't as good as something similar that was posted a week earlier, it's unlikely to make it very far. Since most of these sites have mechanisms to lower the ranking of your content (such as the "bury" button on Digg), you need to have more than just numbers.

Experiment with different kinds of content on each site. What does well in one place might not become a hit on others. Keep track of which content does well where for future reference. Once you get a handle on where the best places are for your specific kinds of content, you can further focus your efforts and get better results with less time invested.

Other Considerations

If you're actively going to pursue making the front page of the major social news sites like Digg or Reddit, you'll need to make sure your hosting is up to the challenge. These sites can send upwards of 50,000 visitors to your site in a very short period of time. If your hosting can't handle the increase in traffic, your site will crash and become unavailable to new visitors. This means a large portion of your hard work will go to waste. Talk to your hosting provider about whether they can handle large bursts of traffic and if they have any suggestions for making your site more able to handle large influxes of visitors.

As we've seen, niche social news sites can send much higher quality traffic to your site than general social news sites. There are some exceptions, though. Sites like Digg and Reddit tend to attract very tech-savvy users. If your niche is technology-related, traffic from these sites can be perfectly targeted for you. And the links you're likely to build through these sites can keep traffic coming to you in the long run.

What You Need to Know

- Social news sites and social bookmarking sites can send thousands of visitors to your blog, website, or other content.
- There are niche social news and bookmarking sites in addition to general ones. The niche sites often send higher quality visitors.
- Investing your time in two or three sites to build up your profile as a power user or influencer can have very positive benefits for your content in the long run.
- Make sure your server can handle the volume of traffic you're likely to get if you reach the front page of one of the major social news sites. If your server crashes, all your hard work will be for naught.

There's More!
Other vital social media stuff

In previous chapters we've discussed the major types of social media: social networks, blogs, microblogs, and social news. These make up only part of the picture, though, when it comes to user-generated content and social media. There are also forums and online listservs, crowdsourcing, presentations and slideshows, document sharing and article syndication sites, online seminars and classes, widgets, and social news releases. And last but not least, there's the prospect of creating your own niche social networking site.

All of these types of social media have one thing in common: they connect people with other people. They allow the sharing of ideas and content between people who might otherwise never connect. Sites like these provide a great avenue for promoting yourself and your message and for attracting new fans.

These alternate forms of social media can be more or less appropriate for your purposes, depending on your niche and your personal goals. If your aim is to engage with others in your niche, forums and groups are likely to be a good fit for you. If your goal is to promote a product, contest, whitepaper (or anything else, really), a social news release or a widget might be perfect for you. Online seminars, slideshows, or article syndication and document sharing might be the way to go if you're trying to establish yourself as an expert and sell a service.

Research the possibilities and decide for yourself which technologies will fit with your goals. There are both paid and free options for almost all of these social media types. Which ones you choose to use depend on your niche and the amount of money you have to spend.

Forums and Online Groups

Forums and other online groups have been around almost as long as the Internet itself. There are forums and listservs for virtually every niche out there, no matter how large or small. Finding them is generally pretty easy, too. There are a few sites that host listserv groups, including Google Groups and Yahoo! Groups. Both are free to use, whether you want to start your own group or join an existing one.

Finding forums is generally as easy as doing a quick search. There are thousands of forums, so spend some time finding the best ones in your niche. Be wary of sites that appear to be unmoderated or filled with mostly spam posts. These sites generally have few users.

There are a few good ways to judge how active a forum is. Look for forums that list the number of members they have and how many members are online at a given time. Check into how old the newest posts are and how many posts are generally updated in a day. You want to join forums that are busy and have an active user community.

Once you join a forum, make sure you read their terms of service and user guidelines. Most forums will allow you to include a link to your website(s) in your signature. The majority of forums do not look kindly on posting commercial links or other spam to their boards. In some cases, though, they have special boards specifically for posting commercial material.

It takes time to become an established member of a forum community. Every forum has its quirks and some are more welcoming than others. Observe for awhile before posting anything. Once you feel comfortable with the way the community works, feel free to start contributing useful information to threads. Start some of your own threads, too, either asking a question or offering up helpful information.

If you consistently provide helpful, useful information in threads, it's likely some forum members will check out the links in your signature. Make sure you indicate what the links are about and that they're links to your site rather than just sites you like. Once you become very established within a community, you can sometimes get away with pushing a bit of your own content once in awhile. But be careful not to break any forum rules and take your cues from other, longer-standing members. If no one else is doing it, it's probably best if you don't either. The last thing you want to do is upset other members and ruin all the hard work you've put in.

Crowdsourcing

Crowdsourcing is the process of inviting others (the 'crowd') to participate in the creation of something. Whether it's a new technology, a business idea, a design for something, or practically anything else, crowdsourcing has become a viable way of getting input from potential customers and others who have a vested interest in refining your idea. It's also probably one of the more difficult social media types to use to promote yourself.

But there are ways you can use crowdsourcing to build your personal brand. Crowdsourcing can be as simple as asking your blog readers to answer a poll question about a decision you're trying to make. It could be an invitation to your fans to design a new logo for you or vote on a few logo concepts you already have.

You might be considering issuing whitepapers or other information products and want to get input on what they should contain.

The best thing about crowdsourcing is that it's a way to interact with your community and get your followers more involved. If you use a website devoted to crowdsourcing to get input, you can even find new followers. And because these new followers have been involved somehow in directing your online activities, they're often more invested in your future success than those who haven't been involved in the process.

Presentations and Slideshows

Sharing presentations online is a great way to attract more followers. You can share videos of presentations you've given on sites like YouTube or other video sharing sites. You can also create slideshows to share on video hosting sites or sites set up specifically for slideshows.

Creating a presentation video or narrated slideshow can further establish you as an expert in your niche. There's likely to be some kind of appropriate slideshow topic no matter what your niche is. Brainstorm the types of information that might be presentable in a slideshow. If you've compiled a list post for your blog, would it work as a slideshow? Could you narrate it and turn it into a presentation? If you're going to use content you already have, try to add some new or extra information. Then link to it from a new post on your blog as well as the original post it came from.

If you're giving a presentation related to your niche, make sure you get someone to record it. If you're using a slideshow, even having an audio recording to dub over the slides is an invaluable addition to your content. If you're offering up new information or content that isn't readily available elsewhere, this kind of media can become viral.

Use as many different outlets for distributing your slideshows and presentations as possible. Put your slides up on one of the many slideshow hosting sites out there. Put your slides and narration or your entire presentation up on video sharing sites like YouTube. Link to each from your blog and website and ask your fans to do the same.

Document Sharing and Article Syndication

There are hundreds of websites out there dedicated to providing useful content to anyone looking for it. Many of these sites allow bloggers and webmasters to use the content for free or a small fee. Others are just distribution points for end-users to read material.

Article syndication sites like E-Zine Articles can be a great way to get your content and your name out there to a large audience. Virtually all of these sites require the people using the content on their own websites to include the attribution information the author of the article has specified (don't deal with sites that don't require this). And in many cases these sites are very well-ranked in search engines, making your content likely to show up on the first page or two in search results. When you combine well-written content with a compelling blurb about yourself in the author information or byline section, it can have a very positive effect on your site's traffic.

Paraphrasing your existing content to create new articles is an easy way to post content on these sites without having to come up with completely fresh information. It also prevents your site from being penalized for having duplicate content (in case search engines decide the article syndication site is the original source instead of your own). Keep your keyword phrases intact within the article but rewrite the whole thing otherwise. Search engines are great at picking up identical and even very similar content but can't detect two phrases with the exact same meaning if they're written differently (at least, not yet).

Document sharing sites like Scribd are similar to article syndication sites in their aim to get your content out to a wide audience. One of the biggest differences, though, is that content is often presented in exactly the format you intend it to (with images, charts, and other information embedded into the format). This is achieved by uploading a PDF or .doc file to share, instead of just copying and pasting text. These sites usually allow their readers to download the content contained on the site in PDF or other universally-readable format.

These types of sites are great if you want to share a sample chapter of a book, a whitepaper, a report on your niche, or other similar content. These sites also work better for longer pieces than do the article syndication sites. Many of those sites limit you to a set number of words (2k-3k in many cases). If your content requires charts, graphs, or other images, these sites are much more suited than most others.

Online Seminars and Classes

Establishing yourself as an expert in your niche is an important step toward gaining Internet fame. Offering an online seminar or class goes a long way toward improving your credibility. Teachers and lecturers are generally given a certain amount of credibility before a person knows anything about you. Having taught a course or seminar is a great addition to your list of accomplishments.

There are a variety of ways to offer online courses. Many experts simply offer emailed lessons on a regular schedule (weekly seems to be the preferred frequency). Others offer a downloadable course in PDF or similar format that includes lessons and worksheets or other materials. Some offer interactive courses with video, audio, text, and other content. Still others offer live courses and seminars where they can interact with attendees.

Teaming up with others to present a panel-style seminar is a great way to network with other leaders in your niche and to draw in more attendees. Everyone benefits because everyone is exposed to new potential fans. Finding others who have complementary skills is even better, as you're less likely to be directly competing with each other. For example, if your niche is website design, maybe you could invite other panelists who specialize in search engine optimization and website copywriting. This way you're all likely to get more readers, as you each offer slightly different content while still being relevant to the majority of each others' readers.

Finding a company willing to sponsor a web class or seminar can be even more useful. In many cases, these companies are willing to pay for advertising or other promotional activities to get the word out. Brainstorm companies that have products related to your niche and the types of web seminars their customers might be interested in. If your niche is, say, digital photography, you might approach a digital camera manufacturer or a photo editing software company to see if they'd be interested in sponsoring. In any case, if they're willing to promote your seminar or class to their email lists and on their website, it can give you a very large potential audience, all interested in what you have to say.

Also brainstorm potential classes or seminars you could host to educate about one aspect of your niche. Recording a seminar and making it available on your website further increases its value. These types of content can become viral and go a long way toward establishing you as an expert in your niche. And if someone has spent the time to take a seminar or class with you, it's very likely they'll remember your name a week or a month later. If your class or seminar is good enough, it's likely you'll get referrals the next time you offer one or offer any other kind of information product.

If you're selling a product or service, consider giving away some freebies to attendees. Offering up one prize for every ten or twenty people who attend can really increase your attendee numbers. If your product is really expensive, maybe just giving away one or even giving away a related product can make a big difference.

Widgets

Widgets are bits of embeddable code made available for anyone to place on their website, social networking profiles, blogs, or anywhere else online. Widgets can be used to promote all sorts of things, from musicians to contests to products. There are a variety of widget platforms out there and sites to help you build your own widgets using a graphical interface with minimal coding required. Most of them support distributing those widgets through various social networking sites as well as on your own website and/or blog.

One of the great things about widgets is that you can use them to spread free tools and other interactive content. If you're an environmentalist, you could build a tool to calculate someone's carbon footprint and put it in a widget. If you're a search engine optimization specialist, you could build a widget to check someone's Google ranking for certain keywords and distribute it via a widget. If you're a musician, you could create a widget that shows one of your music videos or plays an MP3 of one of your songs. Whatever your niche is, there's likely some kind of simple tool you could build that would be useful to your potential fans.

Even if you just have a whitepaper you want to promote or a contest you're looking to get more entries for, building a widget or a badge for others to post on their blog or social networking profiles can work well. Try offering the widget to people after they've signed up for something or otherwise expressed interest. Simply asking your readers and fans to help promote your content can have remarkable results.

Social News Releases

When dealing with traditional media outlets like newspapers or magazines, press releases are a common way of trying to attract media attention. Press releases are typically sent out whenever something newsworthy happens at a company. And they're only sent to select media contacts or through traditional newswire sources. Then the reporter or whoever receives the press release determines whether it's actually newsworthy and, if it is, rewrites the content contained in the release to create an article suitable for their publication (or a news broadcast).

But social news releases (also called "social media releases") are different. They're specifically crafted to attract attention from end users. Media contacts are not the targeted audience for these types of releases. Social news releases often contain multimedia content, including video and audio content, photos, and links to social bookmarking and social news sites. There are distribution services for social news releases that specialize in getting your release out to online news sources (most notably, Google News) and other websites. Two options include PitchEngine, which has paid and free offerings, and Pressitt, a free creation and distribution service.

Another big difference between social news releases and press releases is that a social news release doesn't require some big, newsworthy event in order to issue one. Anything you want to notify your readers, customers, or potential fans about can be social news-worthy. If you've just put up an important new article on your blog, issue a news release. If one of your YouTube videos is rising quickly in the charts or is featured on the home page, issue a news release. Was your blog mentioned on a big-name blog in your niche or in the mainstream media? Issue a news release! Did you just get your one millionth RSS subscriber (or you 10,000th or your 1,000th)? Issue a news release!

Anatomy of a Social News Release

Most social news releases share a few common elements with regular press releases. At the top you should list your contact information, including your website and blog URLs and email address. You may want to include a phone number and/or your Skype address.

After your contact information you need to come up with a title. Remember that your headline should be written with your target audience in mind, not the media. Think about what your fans stand to gain from the information you're providing. Build your headline around what the benefits are to them. You may want to follow your headline with a list of the main points contained within the release. A bulleted list works well for this, as does a numbered list.

The text you include in the social news release should be written with your potential fans in mind. Regular press releases are often written in "marketing-speak" with media contacts in mind. Your social media release should be written as you would write a blog post or article. Maintain the same voice and tone you use in all your other online activities and maintain your online persona. Focus on what you're offering to your readers and what they're going to get out of the information you're providing. Treat this content like any other content you write to help your fan base.

In addition to the standard text information you'll want to provide to readers, consider what multimedia content you want to include. Many distribution services allow you to include YouTube or other online videos, photos, and sound clips. Make sure you have the right to distribute any content you use. This means it either needs to be content you've created, content released under a Creative Commons license, or content you've received permission to use from the content creator.

Once you've finished the content portion of the release, you'll need to add the social media elements. Make sure you include links to vote your content up on all the popular social news and bookmarking sites. Include links to allow readers to post to social networking sites like Facebook and MySpace, too. And don't forget to include links to your website, blog, social networking profiles and pages, and any other pertinent social media sites you belong to.

Tags for including your content on sites like Technorati should be included somewhere. Follow good SEO practices when writing your release. Make sure you link relevant keywords and phrases to your blog or website within the text of the release.

Once your news release has been issued, you should post a link to it on your social networking profiles. Ask your friends and followers to share the link with their friends, too. Post to your microblog(s) and ask your followers to repost your content. Go to every social media and bookmarking site linked to in your release and submit your content. This way when your followers go to vote it up or bookmark it, they won't be met with a page asking them to submit new content (since some might be pressed for time and won't bother).

Other Social Media Opportunities

Social media is still growing, with new opportunities and technologies emerging every day. Keep up to date on what's going on in the social media sphere and be ready to pounce on new technologies that fit within your social media promotional plan. If you're lifecasting, make sure you keep up with similar technologies and what others are doing within the existing platforms. If you're focusing on blogging, be aware of what other bloggers both in and outside your niche are doing and be ready to jump on or even create new trends.

Keep an eye out for the trendsetters in your niche and within the technologies you use. By following what they're doing, you can be an early adopter and sometimes even get publicity for jumping on bandwagons early on.

What You Need to Know

- There are forums and listservs for virtually every niche out there.

- Forums and listservs can be a rewarding, if time-consuming, method of promoting yourself within an established community.
- Crowdsourcing is a great way to engage with your community and make your fans feel more involved.
- Creating presentations and slideshows to share with your fans is a great way to establish yourself as an expert.
- Using document sharing and article syndication sites to distribute your content can help you reach a much wider audience and improve your search engine optimization.
- Offering a useful online seminar or course can add more to your credibility than almost any other online activity.
- Widgets are a perfect way to make content go viral.
- Social news releases are different from regular press releases and optimized to get more attention through social media outlets rather than traditional news sources.
- Keep an eye out for new social media opportunities and technologies that fit within your niche and your Internet Famous strategy.

Strategy

Including shameless self-promotion, but with class!

By now, you should have a good idea of the types of social media platforms available. You've probably also got some idea of which ones are appropriate for your niche. When crafting your social media plan, you'll want to consider all of the platforms out there before choosing which ones are best suited to your goals, abilities, and the time you have available.

At the bare minimum, there are a few technologies you'll absolutely want to use. Blogs are at the top of the list. You'll also want a profile on at least one social networking site. My personal favorite is Facebook for general social networking. Consider your target fan, though. If your target fan is involved in the business community you may want to use LinkedIn; if your target fan is into the indie music scene or a teenager, MySpace may be better suited. In addition to social networking and blogging, social news and bookmarking sites and microblogging are important ways to get your content and yourself out there.

Whichever platforms you decide to use beyond these basics largely depend on your niche and how much time you're willing to commit to becoming Internet famous. You may want to take a month or two to experiment with different social media platforms to see which ones have the highest rewards for the time invested.

The key to social media is the "social" portion of the phrase. Social media is all about interaction. Choosing your social media platforms carefully ensures you'll be better able to engage with the community and build a larger, more involved fan base. If you stretch yourself too thin, you won't be able to communicate effectively with your fans and potential fans. It's better to be very active on a handful of sites than barely active on twenty or thirty.

Initial Considerations

Before you start, you'll want to get an basic idea of which technologies to use. As already mentioned, social networking and blogging are indispensable if you expect to gain Internet fame. But maybe you're trying to decide if you should focus mostly on podcasts within your blog. Maybe you're leaning toward vlogging. Or maybe you want your blog to be a photoblog with minimal text.

Suppose your blog will serve merely as the aggregation point for all the other media you engage in online. You might choose to focus on YouTube or another video sharing site to get your content out. Or Flickr might be more up your alley for posting an ongoing photostream of your life or your work. Maybe you've decided to make the ultimate commitment to becoming an online celebrity and are setting up your own lifecasting channel. Whichever the case may be, deciding on the overall technologies is the first step in crafting your social media marketing plan.

Consider what you really want to get out of your social media experience. If you're looking for general fame, you'll need to direct your focus to much bigger sites than if you're looking to become famous within a very specific niche. If you're pushing a product or service, make sure you choose social media platforms that make sense for your market. Just because you *can* set up a social network or a Facebook fan page for your product doesn't necessarily mean you *should*. Think about why your target audience would want to engage with your company on that kind of channel. If you can't think of a specific reason, it's probably best to skip that particular platform. In other words, if you can't offer something useful on a given platform, then it's probably best to skip it. Simply setting up a page to sell your product or yourself isn't going to cut it in most cases.

Researching appropriate platforms doesn't need to be a chore. Start by doing a quick search for social networking sites in your niche. At the same time, look for social news and other social media sites for your niche. Keep a list or bookmark each site that looks like it might be a good match. Once you have a list of all the sites you feel might be appropriate, it's time to go a bit more in depth.

Start by looking through the site. If there are forums or discussion boards, see whether they're filled with relevant conversations. If they're filled with spam or trolls, it's probably best to move on. Check to see how often things are being updated. Are there regular updates among members? Does the home page provide a news feed showing site-wide activity? Are members actively engaging with one another?

Once you've determined how active the community is and the quality of the content being shared, it's time to do a little off-site research. How many visitors is the site actually getting? While there's no perfect way to get information like that, there are a couple of sites that seem to have fairly accurate traffic data on most major sites. The two sites I turn to are Compete and Quantcast. Compete makes it easy to compare traffic numbers and growth patterns between sites, while Quantcast offers more in-depth demographic information about sites. I usually check both, in case the numbers are significantly different (which doesn't happen very often). Again, what you do with this information will depend largely on your goals and the size of your niche. If your niche is relatively small, a few thousand active visitors a month might be just fine.

Blogging-Based Strategy

Blogging is really the backbone of social media. There are tens of millions of blogs out there (possibly even hundreds of millions) covering every topic imaginable. Whatever your niche is, there's likely already a blog out there covering it.

So if there are so many blogs out there, why on earth would you want to start another one? Wouldn't it just get swallowed up among the millions of other blogs? Wouldn't it get lost in the shuffle and never be seen?

Not necessarily. While there are millions and millions of blogs out there, most of them are either a) very low quality; b) completely neglected by their owners; or c) set up purely as a money-making scheme with spam and/or stolen content. If you set up a blog focusing on providing valuable content on a regular basis, has a professional design (a design that makes it easy for content to be found and read both by search engines and real people), and doesn't hijack other people's content, you'll already be ahead of 99% of existing blogs.

If blogging is centerpiece to your social media strategy, there are a few things you'll want to do from the start. Make sure you claim your blog on Technorati right away. This allows you to track information about your blog and, if you set up multiple blogs in the future, it allows users who like one of your blogs to easily find your others.

Make sure whatever theme you choose is going to be SEO-friendly and will work with the types of content you want to use. If you plan to incorporate videos into your posts on a regular basis, make sure the main content area is wide enough to accommodate YouTube videos (or whichever other video sharing site you plan to get your content from). If you want to include lots of photos, opt for a wider main content column to allow your photos to be displayed easier.

Social news sites can be a blogger's best friend when it comes to promoting content. Sign up on all the major, general social news sites (Digg and Reddit especially) and the major social bookmarking sites (primarily StumbleUpon and Delicious). Start using these sites even before you start blogging. Become a part of the community on each site and contribute content on a regular basis (whether it's your own or someone else's).

Make sure that every time you post something on your blog, you send out a message to your social network friends and your microblogging followers. This alerts those who have already told you they're interested in what you have to say that you've provided some fresh content. Ask your followers and friends to redistribute your content to their friends and followers, too. Doing this can quickly expand your readership and fan base.

Consistency is one of the most important aspects of a successful blog. You need to make sure your tone is consistent across posts. You need to post on a regular basis, whether that's a few times a day or once a week. And you need to keep the format of your blog consistent (i.e., if you start out posting a photo or other multimedia element in every post, you need to keep it up).

If you do want to make changes to the frequency or formatting of your blog, there are a couple of ways to go about it. You can either make an announcement about the change and set a date for when it will take place, or you can gradually make changes and hope no one notices. Whichever one you choose is up to you, though the first option is generally best for major changes.

Suggested Technologies for a Blog-Based Strategy
- The blog platform of your choice. WordPress and MovableType/TypePad are highly recommended.

- Accounts at prominent social networking sites. Sign up for accounts on the appropriate big three sites (Facebook, MySpace, and LinkedIn) as well as any niche social networks.
- At least one microblog. Whether you choose Twitter or Plurk or another microblogging platform, sign up for at least one.
- Accounts on the major social bookmarking and social news sites. You should sign up for accounts on the major sites like Digg, Reddit, and Delicious, as well as any that specialize in your niche.

Multimedia-Based Strategy

Multimedia content is a great way to get yourself out there. YouTube has launched plenty of online celebrities, as have sites like Justin.tv and Revver. Obviously a multimedia strategy works well for certain people. If you're an indie film producer, a photographer, or a musician, a multimedia approach to becoming Internet famous is fitting. But even if your niche is completely unrelated to film, photography, or audio content, there are plenty of ways to employ those kinds of content in your social media campaign.

There are loads of multimedia options available, including video, podcasting, lifecasting, and photo sharing. You can opt to use one technology, all of them, or in any combination. You'll still need a blog to aggregate all of your multimedia content. You should also join the major social networking and social news sites.

Good video and other multimedia content tends to do very well on social news and bookmarking sites. Establishing a presence on these sites is just as important with a multimedia strategy as it is with a blog-based strategy.

Suggested Technologies for a Multimedia Strategy

- You'll still need some kind of blogging platform for aggregating your content and providing a sort of "home base" for your fans to come to. Blogs also help with search engine optimization and branding. You may be able to get by with a blogging service like Tumblr for this kind of campaign, though.

- Set up accounts at all the prominent social networking sites, both the mainstream ones and ones specific to your niche.
- A microblog is another great way to let your followers and fans know about content spread across multiple channels.
- Be sure to set up accounts on all of the major social bookmarking and social news sites, including Digg, Reddit, and Delicious, plus any appropriate niche sites.
- Accounts on video and photo sharing sites like YouTube and Flickr. Be sure to fill in all of your profile information to maximize your branding and to make it easier for your fans on these sites to find your other multimedia content.
- If you use Twitter, you'll likely want to use TwitPic or yfrog to share your photos.

Your Social Media Schedule

Coming up with a schedule for your social media strategy can go a long way toward making sure it doesn't completely consume your life. After all, if you have no life, will you have anything interesting to blog about? Consider how much time is necessary for each type of social media in order to achieve the results you want and then determine whether it's worth the effort.

Take a critical look at your schedule and plan out how much time you can devote to your social media pursuits. If you can only spare an hour a day for all of your social media activities, you'll need to budget your time efficiently.

If your blog isn't dependent on breaking news, prewriting your weekly content is a great way to save time. Writing a handful of posts on a Sunday afternoon (or any other day of the week) and scheduling them to go up periodically throughout the week is generally more efficient than sitting down for fifteen or twenty minutes every day (at minimum) to write a post. Writing four or five posts may only take you an hour or two if you plan out what you want to write or use an editorial calendar to provide a structure for your content.

Schedule a few minutes each day for participating on social news and social bookmarking sites. Engage with other members, leave some comments, and vote up or down other people's content. Make sure to submit some of your own content while you're there, too.

Updating your microblog should be done on a regular basis throughout the day. Installing tools that allow you to post from your browser or mobile device without having to visit the site help to maintain a constant presence without having to log into the site constantly or even to touch your computer.

Social networking sites can be the biggest drains on your time. Conversing with your friends and fans on these sites can take up huge chunks of time if you let it. If you have a set amount of time available to you for your social media efforts, consider visiting your social networks last, after you've already completed your other social media tasks. This way, if you end up spending more time than planned, at least you aren't taking away from other, equally important engagement activities.

Let's say you have an hour each day for social media tasks. Your schedule might look something like this:

- Minutes 1-15: Write blog post for the day; if you've prewritten posts, take a few minutes to engage with commenters.
- Minutes 16-30: Check out social news and bookmarking sites, submit content, comment on the content of others.
- Minutes 31-40: Update status on microblog; engage with followers.

- Minutes 41-60: Check out social networking sites and engage with fans and followers.

If you have more flexibility in the amount of time you spend on your social media efforts, you might choose to stick to a schedule more like this:

- Blog postings: done on a daily basis, or at least scheduled for daily postings.
- Other blog activities (checking comments, etc.): done on a daily basis, or as needed with email notifications.
- Social news sites: visited on a daily basis.
- Social bookmarking sites: visited on a daily basis and updated through browser toolbars.
- Microblog: updated on a continuous basis throughout the day as time allows.
- Social networking sites: visited at least a few times a week and preferably on a daily basis to maintain your presence.

Using tools that allow you to engage with your social media audience from a mobile device can go a long way toward improving your efficiency and effectiveness. Mobile updates allow you to maintain a continuous presence with your fans, making it more likely they'll stay engaged with you and what you're offering.

A Sample Social Media Marketing Plan

There is no one set social media marketing plan that will work for everyone. The possibilities are simply too vast and the uses too varied. No matter what your goals are for social media, there is a platform out there that will help you to achieve those goals. Here is an example of a social media marketing plan based on using as many platforms as possible to achieve the highest recognition in the shortest time period.

First Steps

Our fictional Internet famous hopeful (we'll call her Alice) will be focusing on the technology sector, primarily in consumer gadgets (especially those suitable for business users). There's a fair amount of competition in this niche, but there are also a huge number of potential fans. For simplicity's sake, we're going to say the primary competition for Alice will be Gizmodo, Engadget, Ubergizmo, and Switched. She checks Quantcast to get traffic statistics for them and sees that each month they're getting 879 thousand, 3.5 million, 305 thousand, and 592 thousand U.S. visitors each, respectively.

One thing you'll notice by looking at the demographic information for these sites, is that each one is visited more heavily by men than by women. According to Quantcast, Engadget visitors are 65% male, Gizmodo's are 64% male, Ubergizmo's are 63% male, and Switched's are 52% male. So Alice decides her best bet for gaining Internet fame is to cater to female gadget lovers.

Now that Alice has her niche well-defined (business women who love gadgets), she can create her strategy based on reaching this specific audience. Alice has already decided that blogging will be the main focus of her campaign. She's already started writing content and has decided to post at least once a day with a goal of three times per day. Her goal is to have twenty blog posts ready to go when her blog launches. In addition to blogging, she'll also create occasional YouTube video reviews and do podcasts on a biweekly basis with roundups of gadget news. She sets up a YouTube account and decides also to set up a Revver account at the same time, to see if she can make any money with her videos. She then sets up an account with Odeo for distributing her podcasts.

The first step Alice needs to take in mapping out her social media strategy is to figure out which social networks are most likely to be used by her target fans. Based on its association with business people, LinkedIn is the most obvious, but she'll also use Facebook, since it has slightly more female visitors than male and has better educated and more affluent visitors than typical sites.

Because of her limited time, Alice decides to stick with these two social networks initially, though she may add other niche sites in the future.

Alice decides to set up a Facebook page to interact with her fans (so she doesn't have to worry about the 5,000 friend limit Facebook imposes on regular profiles) and she sets up a group for female gadget lovers. She decides to wait to publicize these pages until she launches her blog. She also looks around for pages and groups related to her niche and joins the ones that look the most active and useful. She spends a few minutes a day contributing to each in hopes of being "friended" by others in those groups.

On LinkedIn, Alice sets up a group for female gadget lovers and starts reaching out to other members who might be interested. She participates in the Q&A section of the site, trying to answer any questions related to gadgets, whether they're posted by women or not (after all, there are likely plenty of women reading these answers).

The next step is to set up accounts on the major social news and bookmarking sites. In addition to Digg, Reddit, and Delicious, she sets up accounts on a technology-focused social news site (Slashdot), and a couple focused on business news (Small Business Brief and Tip'd). She immediately starts commenting and voting on the content of others on all of these sites.

Finally, she sets up accounts on Twitter and Plurk. Alice isn't sure which one she wants to use, as she's heard good things about both, so she decides to experiment with both until one comes out the clear winner (either in terms of increased traffic to her blog or increased visibility in general). She makes a commitment to update each a half-dozen times a day, both with links to her own blog and content as well as relevant content from other sources.

Putting It All In Practice

Alice launches her blog with twenty articles already published. She uses plugins and widgets to make it easy for her readers to submit her content to social news and social networking sites. She only activates the buttons to submit to sites where she's active, in hopes of consolidating votes among just a few sites where she's likely to do well. She also includes buttons in her sidebar for joining her Facebook group and page, joining her LinkedIn group, following her on Twitter and Plurk, and for contacting her.

On the same day her blog launches, she starts publicizing the group and page she'd set up on Facebook. She sends out a link to each to her group of personal contacts through the site and asks them to share the content with their friends. She creates a few updates on her page with links to the articles she's trying to publicize and posts on the group's wall about those same articles. She also contacts the administrators of the groups she belongs to related to her niche to see if she can post a link to her new blog on the group forums or wall. This is the appropriate way to publicize her content, unless the group has a specific policy and place already dedicated to these types of posts. Because Alice has plenty of valuable content already up on her blog and has been an active community member for a number of weeks, many of the administrators are happy to include her link in their regular notifications to group members.

She immediately submits her best content from among those twenty posts to the social news sites she's been active on. She microblogs the URLs of those posts, too, and uses hashtags and carefully selected keywords to optimize them. Alice checks the trending topics on Twitter each day to see what types of content related to her niche are hot. On a given day those keywords might relate to specific products, gadgets in general, or female business people. She specifically asks her followers to repost the content. Of course, at the beginning, Alice has very few followers. Now that she has some useful updates posted, she sets about finding some followers. The first thing she does is look for businesswomen who are likely to be interested in gadgets. There are a variety of different Twitter search tools you can use to find followers within a certain demographic. She follows all of the women who she thinks are a good fit with her target audience, in the hopes they'll follow her back. What she doesn't do is randomly follow a bunch of people who may or may not be interested, in hopes of just getting a huge number of followers. Alice's goal is to get targeted followers who are likely to become fans and re-publicize her content.

If Alice is lucky, at least one of her articles will end up going to the front page of the news sites she's active on. If this happens, she'll almost certainly get thousands of new visitors and tons of new incoming links. This kind of exposure early on can have a huge effect on her site's ability to grow quickly and consistently.

Alice's Social Media Schedule

Alice has one hour a day to spend on social media on Monday through Friday, and can spare three hours a day on the weekends. Here's what her social media schedule looks like:

- **Blog Updates**: Reviews and tips are written on Sunday and scheduled for the week. Each day a few minutes is spent on news update posts. She also checks in on comments in need of moderation once a day (she requires first-time commenters to have their comment approved before it goes live on the site to help prevent SPAM).
- **Microblogging**: Alice has an application installed on her Blackberry for updating her microblogs and does so throughout the day, spending a total of fifteen or twenty minutes a day on these activities.
- **Social News and Bookmarking**: She spends twenty minutes each day on social news and bookmarking sites, submitting her content and commenting on the content of others.
- **Social Networking**: She spends a half hour each day on her own groups (Facebook and LinkedIn) and page. On the weekends she spends a couple of hours participating in other groups. Each day she checks in on the LinkedIn

Q&A section and spends ten or fifteen minutes answering questions.

- **Video Sharing**: She spends every other Saturday creating content for her video reviews. She puts these up on Monday mornings.
- **Podcasting**: Alice creates her podcasts on the Saturdays she's not working on her videos. These are posted every other Wednesday.

Alice has a very full schedule for her social media campaign, but she finds most of the activities to be fun. Interacting with her fans is enjoyable and she often finds herself spending more time on these pursuits on some days. But because she is so engaged with her followers, many of them recommend her site to their friends. Some also suggest post ideas and offer to do reviews for her in exchange for a link back to their own blogs.

Ongoing Efforts

Alice updates her blog every day with at least one post. She starts with a regular posting schedule, offering up reviews on Monday, Wednesday, and Friday and user tips on Tuesdays and Thursdays. She also posts product announcements and news on a daily basis. Her readers know what to expect from her each day and also know that new content is added on a daily basis, making them more likely to check in at least once a day. She posts to her microblog every time she does a blog update, as well as posting links to useful content from others. She also submits her major posts to social news and bookmarking sites.

After a week, Alice posts her first podcast. Two days later she puts up a video review of a new smartphone on YouTube. She also does a photo-rich post reviewing the phone and links the two together. She submits the video and the blog post to the social news and bookmarking sites, and asks her followers on Facebook and her microblogs to go vote (and she provides links to do so).

By keeping up a regular schedule of blog posts, podcasts, and video reviews, Alice keeps her regular readers coming back on a consistent schedule. If readers know their favorite content will be posted on Wednesday mornings, they'll be sure to check in on Wednesday morning. Make sure if you have a regular posting schedule you stick to it. If your readers are constantly expecting things to be there and they're not, they're likely to come to your site less frequently.

Measuring the Results

One of the most important parts of social networking is tracking of the results of your efforts. If you don't keep track of what's working, where you're traffic's coming from, and what kinds of content are your most popular, you'll have a very hard time reproducing success and improving upon what works. By not tracking the results of your efforts, you're likely to waste a lot of time on things that just don't work for you.

Alice has installed Google Analytics to track her progress. She checks on a daily basis for other blogs that send her big spikes of traffic. She sees which of her articles are the most popular among each of her social media channels. She sees which of her social media efforts are sending her the most traffic and which ones aren't working.

As Alice finds out which strategies are working and which ones aren't, she refocuses her activities so she doesn't waste time. By eliminating those tactics which aren't proving fruitful, Alice can grow her traffic even more. She'll have more time to spend on those sites that are sending her traffic if she's not wasting time on those that don't. Be ready to adjust your strategy as your site grows. Things that work one month may not work as well the next. You should constantly be on the lookout for new opportunities to publicize your content.

Developing Your Plan

Based on what you've just read, you should have some idea of how to create your own social media marketing plan. It doesn't need to be complex; notice that the plan above contained no pie charts or spreadsheets. It's just a little basic research and then some ongoing maintenance and tweaking.

If you need to, write your schedule and your social media activities down in a planner (or in an online calendar). This way you'll have a reminder of what needs to be done each day until you form habits. After a few weeks, you'll likely know exactly what needs to be done each and every day.

Make sure you learn how to use your analytics software of choice. Being able to understand the information it presents is incredibly valuable to your social media strategy. Plus, if you don't know how to use it, how will you ever know how many fans you actually have?

What You Need to Know

- Creating a social media marketing strategy doesn't need to be complicated.
- Take the time to research your social media platforms of choice.
- Become an active member of the communities you join.
- Use a good analytics program to track your progress and the success of your efforts.
- Don't be afraid to abandon strategies that just aren't working.

Best Uses

How to not look like a dork

N
ow that you've got a good foundation of knowledge about social media and how to use it to become an online celebrity, and you have a plan on how you're going to use those platforms and technologies to achieve your goals, it's time to look into the absolute best practices for making the most of your social media campaign. There are at least a million different ways out there to use social media. Almost every person out there uses it just a little bit differently than the person before them. And because social media is constantly evolving, what works today might not work tomorrow.

But there are some things that remain consistent no matter which social media platform you're using or what year it is. There are certain guidelines that are a good idea to at least keep in mind when using these sites. Again, they're guidelines, not rules. There is no social media police out there that will come and arrest you if you don't follow these guidelines. They're mainly here just to get you thinking about the best way to use the social media tools available to you.

Engage with Your Audience

Being engaged with your social media friends and followers is one of the most important parts of becoming an online celebrity. Use social media to start a conversation with others. Ask questions of others in your niche. If they ask questions, try to answer them. Ask the opinions of your followers or offer up your opinion on a topic related to your niche. In general terms, engaging with your audience means acknowledging their presence and allowing them to have some influence over your online activities. If you ignore your audience, it's unlikely you'll ever turn them into fans. But by engaging with them, you make them more involved in your digital life, and more likely to become fans and even evangelists for what you're doing.

Listen to What Others Are Saying

This one is similar to engaging your audience, but it revolves around a much larger sphere of social media users. This has more to do with listening to the social media community as a whole. What's bugging people? What are the hot trends and current events people are talking about? What is the general feeling in the world of social media (or at least the part of it you inhabit)? By listening to what's going on around you, you're more likely to be at the forefront of your niche and social media as a whole. And by being a leader and trendsetter, you're more likely to get attention from other bloggers and leaders within your niche— attention you might otherwise miss out on. There are a few ways to collect this information, but one of the easiest ways is to check out the trending topics on Twitter. This gives you nearly real-time information on what's currently being talked about online from all over the world.

Reach Out to Other Users

Being an active member of any social media community means reaching out to other users. Whether they're competitors or not, you should make contact with others working in and around your niche. For a blogger this might mean offering up plenty of links out to other useful blogs. Mention other helpful groups and people on your social networking pages. Don't be afraid of losing readers and fans. If you're providing good content, your fans will keep coming back to you no matter how many outgoing links you provide. And by freely linking to others, you're more likely to get more incoming links.

Other ways of reaching out might be to coordinate or otherwise participate in group projects. Bringing together a number of leaders within your niche for a group blogging/vlogging/podcasting event is a great way to reach out to both them and their followers. Maybe you want to organize an event in the real world such as a conference. If you have good relationships with others in your niche, finding people to help you in these endeavors should be a cinch.

Be a Real Person

I'm going to let you in on a little secret: no one is upbeat and chipper all the time. Likewise, no one is a complete asshole *all* the time (well...). If your goal is to become Internet famous (which it should be, since you're reading this book), you need to be genuine. You need to come across as a real, living, breathing human being. Otherwise, you risk looking like a plant, someone who is only a caricature and doesn't exist in real life. Some people may doubt your motives and wonder if you're affiliated with any business or organization you ever talk about. That's fine if you're actually associated with an organization or business; if you are, you should be upfront about it.

Let your fans and followers in on what's going on in your life, even just a little bit. You're not just some talking head. You're a person with opinions, likes, dislikes, fears, hopes, goals, and so much more. While you don't need to share the minutiae of your daily life or anything too personal, allowing a glimpse into your actual life goes a long way toward better engaging with your fans. It allows them to relate to you on a level they can't with many others in the social media realm. That gives you a big advantage.

Be Honest

This one ties into being a real person. Be honest with your fans and followers. Don't lie to them and don't try to deceive them. Don't be underhanded. Doing any of those things can very quickly turn people against you. If you can't tell your fans the truth about something, don't mention it at all. Lying by omission is the one acceptable form of lying in social media. It's fine to keep things private. But if someone asks you a specific question, it's better to say something like, "I don't feel comfortable answering that," than to lie to them.

Lies have a way of catching up with you. Even if you get away with it in the short term, eventually, someone, somewhere, will figure out you've lied. And then you may be in for some backlash like you've never seen before. Most people on the Internet, as in real life, don't take kindly to being deceived. Remember that whenever you're considering telling a lie, no matter how harmless you think it might be.

Be Respectful

Have some respect for other social media users. Didn't your mother ever tell you, "if you don't have anything nice to say, don't say anything at all?" While you might not need to go that far, make sure that even if you're being negative or otherwise not-so-nice, that you at least remain respectful. We're all human beings. The person you're ranting and raving about (or to) is a real person with feelings. Think about how your actions might affect their day. And think about how you would want someone to treat you in the same situation. If you give respect, you're much more likely to get respect.

The thing is, you tend to get further when you have a respectful, intelligent debate with others instead of just flying off the handle. If you're so sure of your opinion or position, find the facts to back it up. Be open to what others are saying and don't jump to conclusions. A lot of things can be misinterpreted online, so just because you're reading something as coming across in a certain way doesn't mean that's what the original creator meant. You don't have the advantage of body language and other non-verbal cues when reading something. They may have written it or otherwise created it with completely different intentions. And if you flip out at them, it may turn them off from ever creating something again.

Be careful saying things you wouldn't say to someone in person. It's easy to shoot off an email or comment without thinking and later regret it. Consider the long-term effects of what you're about to say, and think about whether you're going to regret it later. In some cases, it's best to type out whatever you want to say and then just delete it. In some cases, that's enough to get it out of your system and then you can communicate in a more constructive way.

Be Consistent

Consistency is one thing that keeps your fans coming back for more. If your content is always of excellent quality, people know what to expect when they visit your site. If you have a certain style in your writing, that's what your readers expect when they come to your blog. And if your videos are always quirky and offbeat, that's what your fans are coming back for.

By maintaining a consistent image online, you make it easier for people to engage with you. Most people are fairly consistent in real life. They act a certain way and those around them know what to expect (most of the time, anyway). While acting out of character once in awhile isn't a deal-breaker, if you're completely unpredictable you're likely to turn more people off than on. Never knowing what to expect is tiring for your fans. Keep that in mind when you're creating new content and figure out if it fits with what you've been doing all along.

Be Transparent

Transparency is tied into the whole honesty thing. Being transparent basically means to disclose any affiliations you might have to your readers. If a company is paying you to write about their product, let your readers know. If you're being paid or given freebies in return for using a certain product (and publicizing your use of it), disclose that somewhere. Most people are fine with product endorsements if you're upfront about what you're doing.

Transparency also means being upfront with the decisions you're making regarding your digital life. While you don't need to share details of things unrelated to your online work, you do need to let people know if you're now publishing articles not written by you, using (and mentioning) podcasting equipment because you're now being sponsored, or otherwise gaining something through your online activities. As with lying to your fans, this kind of thing tends to come out in the end if you try to cover it up.

It's Not All About You!

Social media is a conversation. It's a two-way communication between people, organizations, and companies. If all you do on your social media outlets is rave about yourself and your product, you're not likely to get very far. You need to offer up valuable content to your fans that isn't just from you.

Take Twitter, for example. There are countless Twitter accounts out there with people basically using it to spam anyone kind enough to follow them. They use the service as one giant billboard for whatever it is they're selling. They don't have conversations. They don't retweet what others are talking about. They don't post links to interesting things they've come across online. They just advertise, sometimes even posting the exact same message over and over again, day after day. And while some of them have built up large followings, I can assure you that 99% of those followers are in no way engaged with them. They never retweet their content. They don't click on their links. And in many cases, the only reason they followed them in the first place is because they were followed first and feel it's the polite thing to do.

Don't be like these people. Use your social media platforms to engage with your followers and have a conversation. By recognizing social media as a two-way street, you're much more likely to have a positive social media experience and build an *engaged* group of fans who will further promote you to their own circle of friends and followers.

Participate! Participate! Participate!

Regular participation is one of the biggest factors in becoming an online celebrity. Joining in the conversations going on online makes you more likely to find new fans and keep those you already have interested in what you're doing. Make it a point to participate on a daily basis on at least some of the social media sites you use. Participate in the rest in a regular fashion, whether it's every couple of days or only once a week.

By participation, I mean commenting on the blogs and content of others, engaging with commenters on your own blog, participating in group discussions and other features on social networking sites you belong to, and regularly updating your status, microblogs, and other similar platforms.

Don't Spam

I've already said that social media is a two-way street. But if you've got all these fans, shouldn't you take advantage of that to sell your product or service? Isn't sending an occasional email just pushing your product okay? After all, these people have already said they're interested by following you, right?

Not necessarily. Just because someone has friended you or followed you or subscribed to your blog doesn't mean they can't change their mind and unfollow, unfriend, or unsubscribe. It's easy enough to do any of those things. If you abuse the relationship you've built with your fans, they're very likely to do just that.

Now, that doesn't mean you can't ever promote your products. But make sure you do so in a way that is helpful and useful to your fans. Offering up a product link in your signature, or in context within great content is fine. Just make sure you're offering up something useful.

Automate, But Carefully

Automating at least part of your social media activities is a great way to save time and be more active online. One of the best forms of automation is to use tools that allow you to schedule your updates to occur at a certain time. Most blogging platforms have this feature built-in. There are tools available for many other sites, too, including Twitter.

Automation does have its drawbacks, though. There are tools out there that allow you to post updates from a single place and have them go out to all of your social media profiles. That works fine unless you have more than one of these tools set up. For example, if you have your Twitter feed post to your FriendFeed, that's fine. But if your Facebook profile then pulls from both your FriendFeed and your Twitter feed, you're going to end up with a lot of duplicate content (and yes, I've seen people who do this, even some big-name social media users).

Align Yourself with Others

Find others in the social media community who are already popular within your niche. Then make friends with them. Comment on their blogs. Engage in their conversations on Twitter and other social networking sites. And basically try to get in their good graces.

The advantage to you in all this is that people judge others a lot based on their associations. If you associate yourself with others, you're more likely to be viewed in the same light as they are. If someone is viewed with an expert and you're seen conversing intelligently with them on a regular basis, you're more likely to be seen as an expert.

Add Value

In every interaction you have online, you should seek to add value. By offering up information that's useful or entertaining, those around you are more likely to remember your contributions. By adding value to the conversation you're more likely to get people to follow your recommendations, click on your links, and otherwise engage with you.

Think about ways to improve the sites you use. Think about ways to offer things no one else is offering. And think about things you can do to make yourself more useful to those around you. All of these things are more likely to establish you as an expert within your niche and garner you more fans.

Don't Ask for More Than You Give

Don't ask your fans to do things for you that you, yourself, don't do for others. If you never retweet the content of others, what makes you think they'll retweet your content? If you never share links from others, why should they share your links? And if you never comment on the blogs of others, why should anyone comment on your blog?

Take the time to participate and engage if you want others to engage with you. It's kind of like the Golden Rule: Do unto others as you would have them do unto you. If you aren't willing to give anything back to the community, don't expect them to give anything back to you.

Use the Tools Available to You

There are a ton of tools out there for automating and organizing your social media efforts. There are even entire browsers (Flock) dedicated to improving your social media experience. Find the tools that allow you to use the social media platforms you've chosen in a more efficient and effective manner.

Take some time to research and try out the variety of tools available. One of the most important kinds of tools you can use to improve your social media experience is to install mobile versions of your social media sites on your cell phone. There are apps available for almost every kind of smartphone or PDA. Using these allows you to update your status and participate in conversations while you're on the go.

Don't Overcommit

This rule applies to a few different things. First of all, don't sign up on too many social media sites. It's better to stand out on two or three than to barely be able to keep up with a dozen. In the beginning you may be tempted to sign up for dozens of sites hoping something will stick. That's fine if you want to do an initial testing period and are willing to devote the time necessary. But plan on scaling those back after a few weeks or a month. Stick with a couple of social networking sites, a couple of social news sites, a blog, and a microblog.

Of course, the less time a certain social media platform takes, the more sites you can join. For example, distributing your videos on a number of sites make sense. After all, the video is the time-consuming part. Uploading it to a half dozen sites doesn't take nearly as long. You can also scale up the number of sites you participate on as your available time increases. If you can spend hours every day online, feel free to sign up for more sites. But if you only have an hour to spend each day, you're likely better off limiting where you participate.

Another rule for this is not to promise things you can't deliver to your fans. If you can't produce a video every week, don't say you will. If blogging on a daily basis is too much for you to handle, then post every other day or twice a week. It's better to produce quality content less frequently than to post useless content every day.

Don't Shy Away From Controversy

Businesses and organizations generally try to stay away from controversy. Not many professionals adhere to the "any publicity is good publicity" model any more. But controversy can get you a lot of interest. Taking a stand on an issue, especially the unpopular position, can bring you tons of traffic. And if you argue your case well and remain respectful of the opposing view, it can even garner you plenty of respect and establish you as an expert.

Joining in existing controversies on other sites is also useful. Engaging in a debate within a forum of social networking group can definitely raise your profile. Leaving comments disagreeing (again, respectfully) with someone else's blog post can get you plenty of traffic linking through from that blog (especially if your comment is near the top). Consider publishing a blog post with an opposing viewpoint and linking through to the original post, too. This works especially well if your comments are longer than what most people will read in a comments section.

Don't Expect Results Overnight

Becoming an online celebrity, like almost any other worthwhile pursuit, is likely going to take some time. You need to be persistent in your efforts and willing to invest months before you're likely to get much traction. Very few people are instant online successes. Even the people who were catapulted into the limelight seemingly overnight with some kind of viral content generally have a dozen or more previous efforts under their belt that got them little or no attention.

Don't give up too quickly on any one social media platform you try. Give it a few weeks or a couple of months even before making up your mind whether something is worthwhile. By consistently participating, you'll continue to gain popularity. And by constantly being on the lookout for opportunities, you may find yourself presented with something almost guaranteed to put you in the position you want to be in. You just have to stick with it long enough to find that particular something.

Don't Be Afraid to Break Rules and Best Practices

This one is probably the most important of all the rules. Don't be afraid to disregard any of these rules. There are plenty of people out there who have become incredibly popular online by breaking any or even all of these rules. Some people really do seem to be assholes all the time. Some people barely ever engage with their followers directly. Some automate so recklessly they end up populating their activity feeds with scores of duplicate entries. And some people ignore everyone else around them and still end up awesomely popular.

So the most important rule is to do what you feel is going to work for you. Be true to yourself and your ideas. If you have an idea that contradicts something here, feel free to try it out. Social media and everything related to the Internet is constantly evolving.

Be ready to evolve with it and change if change is necessary. You never know—you may stumble across something that works spectacularly for you.

What You Need to Know

- The way you communicate with those around you on social media sites has a huge impact on how popular you become.
- Realize it's not all about you and that your fans don't want to be bombarded with advertisements for you, your business, your product, or your service.
- Be willing to invest the time to make social media work for you and don't expect results overnight.

Online Reputation
Protect it like your first-born child

As your Internet fame grows, you'll almost certainly be met with issues regarding your online reputation. Some people love to stir up controversy and often do so by targeting those who are successful. And sometimes people have legitimate complaints against you, whether you intentionally did anything wrong or not (I'm hoping not).

Tons of people have been humiliated online. It happens every day and in almost every medium. Whether an embarrassing video ends up passed around about you (as happened to Miss Teen South Carolina after she gave an unintelligible answer on stage during the Miss Teen USA pageant) or you make an ass of yourself by lying or otherwise getting facts wrong (as has happened to countless bloggers out there), humiliation and Internet fame go hand in hand. Unfortunately, these types of situations are almost impossible to avoid once they get out. Once a video or other content goes viral, slowing it down or stopping it can be nearly impossible.

And then there are those cases when someone is maliciously attacking you, whether justified or not. Everyone has the right to express their opinion, online or off. You can't stop someone from calling you a jerk on their blog. But that doesn't mean you have to just sit back and take it without doing something to mitigate the effects.

So what do you do when someone is suddenly calling your motives, your intelligence, your expertise, or anything else about you into question? There are a number of strategies you can employ to manage your reputation online. Some are more or less effective against different kinds of attacks on your reputation. And sometimes, there's not much you can do when someone attacks you (but we'll get to how to deal with that, too).

The First Step is Prevention

It's a lot easier to prevent bad publicity than it is to counter it. Your focus initially should be on preventing negative things from being said about you. There are a few ways to go about this. The first is to make sure your own content is appearing in search engine results and on social networking and news sites. Make sure everything you do online is optimized with the keywords and phrases you've chosen, whether on your website or blog or on social networks.

Register for accounts with all of the major social media platforms as well as every social media site you think you might want to use in the future and any that are related to your niche, whether you intend to use them or not. This ensures that your chosen screen name and other information are reserved for you and can't be used by someone looking to damage your reputation. It's very easy for someone else to register on a site with the screen name you generally use and then post false information or otherwise make you look bad.

Remember that everything you do online is out there forever. Even if you delete a blog post, a video, or some photos, it's likely there's a cached version somewhere. You need to be exceedingly careful of what you post online, whether in the form of photos, videos, or even blog posts. Make sure whatever you put out there is something you won't regret in a month, or a year, or ten. There are services out there that can help to get rid of content you don't want available to the world, but it's not always possible to get rid of everything, especially if someone has already found it and re-posted it to their own blog or website.

Take advantage of privacy settings on the social networks and other sites you use. Fine-tuning who can see your notes, photos, videos, and other updates can go a long way toward preventing certain content from becoming public without limiting what you can share with close friends. Be careful of the terms of service on a site, though, as sometimes they can use any of your content in advertising or other promotion (meaning even if you've set something to private, they have the option to publicize it in promotional materials).

Be careful of posting things online in the heat of the moment, too. If you're angry or upset about something, you may act in a way you wouldn't normally and you may say things you later regret. It's fine to be emotional and can add a great deal of depth to your online personality, but be careful of being too emotional or irrational. Write or record your rant in the heat of the moment (preferably in a program outside the one you'd be posting in so you don't accidentally hit submit instead of cancel), but wait until you have a clear head before publishing it for the world to see.

The same can be said for posting things while under the influence. Posting something while drunk can be something you come to regret the following day. Consider leaving your cell phone or other mobile device at home if you know you'll be drinking or otherwise intoxicated. Just take a camera with you so you can still get photos (to review and upload later). Of course, this is one of those things that depends on what kind of persona you're portraying. Drunk tweeting or otherwise posting while you're under the influence can add to your persona if that's the kind of image you're after.

But what are you supposed to do if someone is saying negative things about you, especially if they have more clout with the search engines than you do? And what about if you did post something you now regret and want to get rid of it? What are you supposed to do then?

Once It's Already Out There

What you do once someone has posted something negative about you largely depends on the nature of what's been posted. If the information posted is inaccurate or false, the first step is to contact the owner of blog site or the person who posted the information. Notify them of the inaccuracies and provide supporting information if you can. Inform them of the actual story, if there is one. If they still refuse to take it down, post a comment on the offending site, explaining your side of things. If that still doesn't work (after all, the site owner can opt to delete your comment if they choose), you can offer your side of things on your own blog or website. Make sure you link to the original material and hope a trackback is allowed on the offending site.

If the information posted about you is defamatory, you can consider contacting the site's host or ISP. Sometimes hosts are willing to take the offending sites down, depending on the nature of the offense. This is something to only use as a last resort, though, and there's no guarantee the ISP will be helpful. As an absolute last resort, consider contacting a lawyer to send a cease and desist letter or taking the offending site to court. This can be a very time-consuming process and is only worth it if the site in question has a large influence over your target audience.

If the information on the site is technically true but not presented in the best light, you should also start by contacting the site owner directly. Give them your version of events and ask if they'll add your side of things to their original post or a linked post. Alternately, you can post your side of things in the comments. Make sure you remain respectful in your communications and add supporting documentation. Don't try to cover up the truth and make sure you're not giving a skewed version of events. There's nothing wrong with defending yourself or giving a more complete version of events if the blogger in question is missing some key piece of information that guided your decision.

Don't be afraid to apologize if you're in the wrong. Explaining your motivations for doing something can sometimes help, but there are times when you just have to sit back and say, "I was wrong and I'm sorry." You'd be surprised at how far something as simple as this can go. In many cases, if you're sincere about wanting to rectify the situation, you can gain a lifelong ally in the person who originally attacked you.

On occasion, you may be attacked by trolls. These people thrive on controversy and flame wars. The worst thing you can do in these situations is respond. If you don't respond, no controversy is created. By ignoring them, you rob them of their power to coerce you. Without a response, they have no fuel to feed their assault and will likely get bored and leave. Trolls can generally be identified by their completely inflammatory remarks and generally abusive comments. Oftentimes these will be made either on a forum you frequent or directly on your blog, video channel, or other public profile. If you have the power to, go ahead and delete the comments where they've appeared, or contact a site administrator and ask that they do so. Realize, though, that this sometimes backfires and makes them all the more likely to keep coming after you. But take comfort in the fact that within a week or so they're likely to find a new target for their attacks and will leave you alone.

Using Negativity to Your Advantage

Sometimes it's best not to run away from bad publicity. If you're careful about how you go about things, you can sometimes take negative publicity and use it to your own advantage. While the old adage "any publicity is good publicity" is going overboard a bit, negative publicity is still publicity. It's still getting your name out there in front of people who might not otherwise have heard of you.

Let's say you've been targeted by an A-list blog much larger than your own as the focus of some negative commentary. How do you use that kind of attention to your advantage? How can you somehow capture some of that blog's audience for your own, further increasing your fan base?

There are a couple of approaches you can use to gain something from this kind of attack, and it largely depends on a couple of factors. First, is the person attacking you right? Are they telling the truth about something? Or are they giving false information, either intentionally or because they have been misinformed? The second reason has more to do with what your goals for being online famous are. If you don't really care much what people think of you as long as they keep coming back for more, then your options are a bit more open. But if you're representing a business, product, or organization, your options are much more limited and you need to take a more delicate approach.

If you're concerned with minimizing damage caused by this kind of attention, you need to take a very careful approach in dealing with the offending site. First, contact the author. Explain to them your side of the story and send any supporting documentation. Ask them to share your side of the story with their readership. Give them a few days to respond. If you don't hear back, consider leaving your side of the story in their comments section. Offer to take the discussion offline, too. Ask them to email you if they'd like to discuss the issue further. This makes you seem like the bigger person.

Now, if the A-list blogger takes you up on the offer to continue the conversation outside of their website, make sure you don't write or say anything you wouldn't want their visitors to read. Don't be surprised if any communication you have is posted publicly for the world to see. This is especially true if you say anything inflammatory or offensive. Don't rant and don't rave. Just keep a clear head and be as concise and accurate as possible in your dealings. Be respectful in your dealings.

Another option is to post a response on your own blog and then comment on the original post. Be sure to provide a link back to the originating post in your own, too. This can end up bringing a lot of new visitors to your site, but be prepared for fans of this other blogger to vehemently defend their preferred blogger, openly and publicly in your comments. Don't ignore these people. For the most part, you want to engage with these people and try to convert them to become your fans. While it's fine to moderate your comments, don't delete a comment just because it's negative. This just makes you look worse in the situation. If you want to delete (or even edit) abusive comments, feel free. But if someone is speaking rationally, leave the comment up and respond accordingly. The goal here is to open up a dialogue and gain some respect for yourself.

Of course, if your primary goal in all this is to just get as much attention as possible, there are other things you can do to maximize the publicity you get. Be forewarned that these tactics are unlikely to put you in the good graces of the blogger in question, and may gain you a lot more enemies than friends. But there are advantages to being hated, mainly that others will likely jump to your defense just to go against what the majority are doing.

If you have a thick skin and are willing to take this through to the end, it can go a long way toward making you an online celebrity. Just be prepared for backlash, trolling, and myriad other attacks against you, your site, your character, and anything else people feel they can attack.

First of all, you want to figure out an appropriate response to the A-list blogger in question. If they were particularly scathing, be just a little bit worse in your response. If they were perfectly respectable in their accusations against you, realize that if you come across as condescending or scathing, you're likely to be hated even more. This can work in your favor by gaining you more attention. It's largely dependent on how comfortable you are with being the "bad guy" in this situation.

So, in forming your response, you'll likely want to start in the comments section of the offending blog. Leave a short response initially, possibly calling into question the original poster's intelligence or character. Don't be abusive, though, as many blogs will just delete an abusive comment (and rightfully so). The next step is to post something on your own blog (or create a video, podcast, or other online response). Post it prominently on your blog so that anyone visiting your site will see it right away.

Engage with the A-list blogger in a way that keeps the conversation (or argument) going. The goal here is to stretch it out for as long as possible and even to try to draw others (particularly other A-listers) into the fight. While the specific tactics you use will be dependent on the tone and content of the original post as well as follow-up comments, your aim should be to keep the other person involved. Don't get too extreme or they may just brush you off as a troll. You need to approach this more like a heated debate than an all-out fight. Be careful to use mudslinging and similar tactics sparingly. Otherwise you may just get blacklisted before you get the kind of attention you seek.

Remember that these kinds of extreme tactics are unlikely to get you many fans from the readership of the blog that originally attacked you. But if you do this right, you should get other bloggers out there to take sides and, with some luck, some other big names may side with you. This is where you're likely to gain new fans and more popularity. Plus, you may find that you've gained some important allies within your niche and the larger online community in the process. Or, you might find that everyone now hates you. But hey, isn't infamy just as good as fame?

The Worst Thing You Can Do

It's in the nature of many people to avoid conflict at all cost. When you're attacked online, your first instinct may be to lay low and wait for it all to pass. That is the worst possible thing you could do. When attacked by someone high-profile (or at least higher profile than you are), realize that their fans are now watching you. They're looking to see how you react to the challenge, and whether you fight back or slink away with your tail between your legs.

This is the time to put out your best content. Whether you respond directly to the attack or not is up to you, but make sure you maintain a presence on your blog, social networks, and anywhere else you're trying to build your popularity. If your content is good, it's likely you'll gain some fans out of the whole ordeal. But if you run from the problem and lay low, not only are you unlikely to gain any new fans, you also might lose some existing ones in your absence.

Keeping Track of Your Reputation

It's almost inevitable that eventually someone will attack you online. But how are you supposed to know when it happens? You can't read every blog out there (and wouldn't want to). You need a way to track what people are saying about you or your company or product without having to manually look for it.

The first thing to do is to set up alerts on both Google and Yahoo!'s search engines. Both sites have a tool to allow you to do this that emails you with updates about your chosen keywords in their search results every day (or more or less frequently as you choose). These are a great start to keeping track of what's being said, but they aren't the only way to do so.

Other specialized search engines, such as Technorati, let you subscribe to an RSS feed for specific search results. Add these to your feed reader within a special folder. Look through this on a daily basis to see what's being said about you. Other services, such as Monitor This, allow you to keep track of search results across multiple search engines through an RSS feed. And there are still other sites out there that let you track what's being said in forums around the web.

Check incoming links and trackbacks on your blog, too. Oftentimes, people will link to the offending material if they're saying negative things about you, giving you immediate access to what's being said. Check these links on a daily basis to be sure incoming links are accurately portraying you and what you're saying. (You should also be checking these to verify no one is using your content in a way you don't approve of.)

Make sure you monitor your reputation on a daily basis. Reacting quickly when something is said is one of the keys to preventing things from being blown out of proportion. By reacting in a timely manner, you're more likely to be looked upon as someone who cares about what is said about themselves online and as someone who is willing to engage with others to make things right if a wrong has been committed.

What You Need to Know

- Reputation management is an ongoing process in maintaining your online celebrity.
- Don't engage with trolls. They're looking for attention and by denying them that they're more likely to leave you alone.
- Make sure you maintain a presence when negative things are being said and all you want to do is run and hide.
- Sometimes you can use negative coverage to your advantage.
- Use the free tools available online to track what's being said about you.

I'm Internet Famous, Now What?

Taking it all off(line)

While Internet fame is great for achieving the aims of many people, what if you want more? What if you want to take that Internet fame and translate it into notoriety in the "real world," the world of the mainstream media?

People have done it, though it doesn't happen often. One notable success is Timothy Ferriss, author of The 4-Hour Workweek, a #1 New York Times best seller. When Tim started promoting his book, he targeted mostly bloggers. He went to conferences bloggers attended. He networked. He granted interviews. And he got a lot of attention. That attention was responsible for catapulting his book onto the Times best seller list and landing him appearances on morning news shows, articles in magazines and newspapers, and otherwise general fame. He maintains his online celebrity, but at the same time he's famous among a lot of circles off-line.

Or maybe you want to engage with your fans offline, in a more personable environment. Participating in conferences and seminars are a great place to start. You could teach a class or guest lecture in someone else's class. You could even organize your own conference or seminar, including others in your niche in the process.

Making the Decision to Take It Offline

The decision to go offline with your fame can be a tough one. There are a myriad things to consider. First of all is why you want to take your fame offline. If you don't have a clear answer for this one, you might be better off to stay online and bask in your fame there. Other things to consider include how to make your first forays into the "real world" and how often you'd like a presence there.

You might start out by attending some industry conferences. This is an easy and fairly low-pressure way to put yourself out there. Make sure you post on your blog, microblog, and social networks that you'll be attending. Live blogging or microblogging from the event is a great way to let fans who might also be there know where you are and what you're up to.

Or you might opt to get attention from the mainstream media. This can be a great way of getting your name out there to a much larger audience. There are opportunities in print magazines and newspapers, on the radio, and on television. And there are a variety of ways to go about gaining a presence in these outlets.

Mainstream Media Attention

Getting mainstream media attention can be like the holy grail for some. In some circles, even if you have hundreds of thousands of fans online, if you have no offline credentials, you aren't taken seriously. So being interviewed or featured in an article by a mainstream magazine or newspaper, or even television or radio appearances, can go a long way toward establishing further credibility.

Don't expect the mainstream media to come knocking on your door, though. Journalists are busy and regularly have hundreds of stories thrown at them every day. You'll need to do something to get their attention—something that sets you apart from everyone else.

Start with an idea. Most journalists won't care about who you are. They care about ideas and about stories. They care about what you can bring to their readers. So start with an angle, something worth writing about. In many cases, this could be a new angle or some original research in your niche. It could be a new product launch or a human interest story (journalists especially like the personal aspect of any story). Whatever it is, realize you need to present it as something unique that no other media organization has covered in the same way before.

Research the media outlets that might be interested in your story. One reason press releases and other media contacts often result in little or no coverage is that the media outlet contacted rarely deals in the type of story they're being presented with. Make sure you get the name of the appropriate person to send your release to in order to further increase your chances at getting coverage. If the wrong person receives it, there's little chance they'll take the time to track down the correct person for that type of story.

Network with journalists at industry events. Let them know you're available if they need an expert within your niche. Be friendly but avoid being pushy. Just give them your business card and tell them to feel free to contact you any time. Don't take up too much of their time, though, as they're likely busy covering the event. A few minutes is generally enough to leave a positive impression. Consider contacting them after the event if you had a particularly good conversation. This can help to cement your place in their mind as an expert within your field

Another option is to pitch writing articles for a publication yourself. If you've been writing on your own blog for awhile, this can be a viable option. Check out the current edition of the

Writer's Market to find magazines that serve your niche and see if they accept freelance articles. Brainstorm article ideas much the same way you brainstorm blog post ideas. And when you have a well-conceived idea, send out a query letter or two pitching your idea. While it can be difficult to get into many magazines, if you're already established online as an expert, you're likely to get further than if you have little or no experience.

Don't discount local media. Freelancers for larger publications often listen to local radio and read local papers. If your story is interesting enough, they may contact you for more information and run a larger piece about you (or at least a piece with a larger audience).

Conferences and Seminars

Attending a conference or a seminar can be one of the lowest-pressure ways of connecting with your fans offline. There are conferences for almost every industry out there, so whatever your niche is you're sure to find at least one. Some conferences are significantly better than others, though, so make sure you research your options before laying out any money to attend.

Once you've decided on a conference, make sure you let your fans know you'll be attending. Post on your social networks as well as your blog that you'll be there and if you'll be attending any particular workshops or speakers. While at the conference, you may want to blog or microblog the event live. This serves two purposes. The first is that this kind of content can go a long way toward getting the attention of other bloggers in your niche. It's likely you'll gain a fair number of incoming links and traffic from people who were unable to attend themselves.

The second reason, though, is so that your fans know where you are and can track you down. Encourage them to approach you if they see you through your regular updates. Make sure you're friendly to everyone who approaches and treat them just as you would someone commenting on your blog or other content.

Maintain your online persona throughout the event to further reinforce your celebrity.

Another option is to actually take out a booth in the vendors area of a conference. This is a great way to make yourself available to fans and works particularly well if you're selling a product or service. If you're going to rent booth space, make sure you take at least one other person with you (to cover bathroom breaks and the like). Be friendly and approachable to all who pass and be sure to conduct yourself in a professional manner.

If you're really lucky, you may be asked to speak at an industry conference based on your Internet fame. Some conferences put out open calls for papers. Take advantage of these and submit something. If well-written and on-topic, these can be a great way to get started in professional speaking. Generally, speaking engagements also come with some form of pay and often free lodgings for the duration of the conference. These kinds of engagements are great in that they also allow you to partake in all the conference has to offer when you're not speaking. Plus, having speaking credentials further increases your expertise and the likelihood of getting new fans in the process.

Make sure when you attend a conference you take plenty of business cards with you. In addition to your name and profession, your business cards should list your website, blog address, and your profile page on any other major sites you're active on. Hand them out freely to anyone you meet at the conference so they may follow you online, making them more likely to become a fan.

Don't overlook small venues for speaking, either. Local and regional clubs and organizations often have meetings or conferences where they invite speakers. Get in touch with organizations related to your industry or niche and see what the opportunities are. While these often don't pay (or pay very little), they can be great exposure and often introduce you to powerful people within your specialty.

Informal Meetups

Maybe you're not interested in doing conferences and seminars. If that's the case, an informal meetup might be a better fit for you. These work especially well if you live in or near a city with a concentration of people within your industry or niche. If your fan base is big enough, any large city is likely going to contain enough of your fans to make a small meetup possible.

Organizing a meetup can be done informally through your blog or using a site dedicated to bringing people together offline, like Meetup.com. If you use your own blog, consider simply putting up a post stating that you're going to be at a certain location at a certain time. Ask your readers to leave a comment if they plan on showing up. Make sure whatever place you choose is going to be large enough to accomodate all who RSVP plus some additional people. A park or other outdoor space might be appropriate for the initial meeting place, with plans to then go get coffee or snacks after everyone has arrived. This way, if you end up with a hundred people showing up, you aren't going to overwhelm your favorite little coffee shop or restaurant.

Have some idea of what you might want to talk about at these informal meetups. The worst possible scenario is that you have tons of fans show up and then have nothing to say. You don't need to have a speech or anything prepared, but come up with ideas for talking points ahead of time so you can get a conversation going.

Things to Beware of When Going Offline

Going offline with your Internet fame is not unlike meeting someone in real life after conversing with them on an online dating site. There are a number of things to keep in mind when meeting people in real life who have been following you online. Here are some guidelines for doing so:

- **Remember that you have little control over who your fans are**. When you make yourself available to your fans offline, you have no control over who shows up. Be aware that your fans may not be what you're expecting. You may be presented with people who are rude, obnoxious, clingy, or worse. Be prepared for this and ready to show the same courtesy to everyone who shows up. These people are your fans and they admire you. Be grateful they made the effort to show up.

- **Similar to number one, you can't delete people offline**. If someone shows up on your blog or other site and starts being abusive or obnoxious, you can delete or block them. This isn't possible in real life. You're going to have to deal with the behavior and attitude of anyone who shows up.

- **Always meet in a public place!** I cannot stress this one enough. If you're going to meet with some fans, make sure you're meeting in a public place where there will be plenty of other people around. Don't ever invite people you don't know to your house or hotel. This is just asking for trouble. While 99% of your fans are probably fine, there's a chance some of them might not be. And even if you're not in any danger, what if you end up with a guest who just can't take the hint it's time to leave? If you're in a public place, it's easy enough for you to leave.

- **Always take a friend with you.** If you're going to be meeting fans in an informal setting, especially, it's important to take someone you know with you. It's the buddy system. If you're at a conference this is somewhat less important, but make sure you don't leave the conference setting with friends you don't know.

- **Let people know where you're going.** Let at least one friend or family member know your plans. If you're going to be at a conference or seminar for an extended period of time, make arrangements to check in regularly. And let your contact person know what to do if you don't check in as scheduled.

- **Have a backup plan.** If you're going to meet some fans in an informal setting, it's a good idea to arrange for a friend or family member to call you a half hour or so after your meeting is to start. This way, if you find that the people who have shown up are making you uncomfortable or you are otherwise unhappy with the situation, you can fake an emergency and excuse yourself from the situation. Try to be a good sport if you can, but if you're really feeling uncomfortable, this makes a good escape plan.
- **Trust your instincts!** If you meet up with fans and are feeling uncomfortable, go with that feeling. Don't meet with anyone who's giving you the creeps online. If you want to get out of a situation for any reason, find a way to get out of it. I'm a firm believer that much of the trouble we find ourselves in in life could be avoided if we'd just trust our gut feelings!

Use your common sense when meeting people offline. While you'll likely find that the vast majority of your fans are perfectly fine people (and you'll probably have a lot in common with them, too), there are bad apples in every group. If you're prepared for this and have a contingency plan, you'll likely get through things just fine.

What You Need to Know

- Participating in conferences and seminars is a great way to meet up with fans offline.
- Mainstream media coverage is often difficult to get, but can increase your credibility in many circles.
- Organizing an informal meetup can be tons of fun and is easy enough to do if you live close to large group of your fans.
- Use common sense when meeting with people offline and make plans for worst-case scenarios.

Glossary

Alt Tags: Also referred to as an "alt attribute," alt tags are used in HTML and XHTML to specify an alternative text to be displayed if an image or other content cannot be shown.

Blog: A blog is a type of website meant to be updated on a regular basis that displays content (posts) in a reverse-chronological order (with the newest content appearing first). Blogs may be personal, topical, news-oriented, or cover just about anything else you could think of.

Creative Commons: A set of licenses content creators can choose from for granting rights to others to use their work. These range from attribution licenses (where the secondary creator needs only credit the original creator) to more restrictive licenses like the "Attribution Non-Commercial No Derivatives" license where others can redistribute content but cannot make changes to it or profit from it.

CSS: Stands for Cascading Style Sheets. CSS is a language for describing and defining the way a web site looks and the way it's formatted.

Hashtags: A hash tag is a word or short phrase used to "tag" an update on sites like Twitter. They're called hashtags because they're preceded by the hash symbol (#).

Linkbait: Linkbait is content on a website created specifically to bait other websites into linking to it. Linkbait is looked down upon by some but can be a valuable marketing tool. To some extent, linkbait is any content that enough people find useful enough to link to.

Lolcat: Lolcats are a meme that originally consisted of photos of cats with captions that generally included the term "lol" (Laugh Out Loud). They have since evolved to include other types of animals and a variety of captions that are generally humorous.

Long Tail: The Long Tail originates from an article Chris Anderson wrote in Wired magazine in October 2004. It originally referred to businesses like Amazon that sell a large number of unique items but each in relatively small quantities. In regards to search engines, the long tail consists of all those phrases on your site that might drive in a few visitors per month, but aggregated together can account for a large percentage of your incoming traffic from search engines.

Meme: Internet memes generally refer to a concept or phrase that spreads rapidly online, through blogs, email, and social networking. Examples of memes include lolcats and Rickrolling.

Meta Tags: Also referred to as "meta elements," these provide metadata about a web page. They include tags in the "head" section of an HTML or XHTML document that specify things like the page description, title, and keywords. Description and title meta tags are important for search engine optimization purposes.

PHP: PHP is a common, open-source web scripting language used to create dynamic web pages.

Plugins: Plugins are bits of add-on scripts and applications that can be included in a website to extend the site's functionality. For example, WordPress has plugins available to prevent spam comments or to include a contact form on your site (among thousands of other plugins).

Podcast: A podcast is a series of audio or video files released in a series, generally covering a specific topic, that are syndicated online. Podcasts are generally subscribed to via programs like iTunes or Juice, and updates are delivered to subscribers automatically.

Self-hosted: Self-hosted, in reference to blogs and other CMSs, means that the website is hosted on your own server, instead of on the servers of the company providing the CMS or blogging platform.

Server: A server is the computer a website (or group of websites) is hosted on.

Vlog: A blog comprised of video content.

Widget: A widget is an element of a website that displays information that can be interacted with by a website visitor. In many cases, widgets can be embedded on multiple websites to allow visitors to interact with centrally-maintained data (such as poll widgets).

Wiki Farm: A wiki farm is a type of hosted wiki service that offers tools to create and develop a number of independent wikis.

List of Websites Mentioned

Throughout this book I've mentioned tons of great websites. But rather than include the website addresses for each of them in the text, I've put them all in an alphabetized list here. It looks a bit nicer this way and keeps the main body of the book a bit tidier.

Alexa: *Website traffic statistics tracker.* http://alexa.com
Authonomy: *Social network for writers.* http://authonomy.com
Bing: *Search engine.* http://bing.com
Blip.tv: *Video host for recurring online shows.* http://blip.tv
Blogspot/Blogger: *Free blog host owned by Google.*
    http://www.blogger.com
BlogTV: *Live video streaming service.* http://www.blogtv.com/
BuddyPress: *Social network plugin for WordPress.*
    http://buddypress.org
Buzznet: *Music social networking.* http://www.buzznet.com/
Compete: Website analytics and tracking information.
    http://compete.com
CNN: *TV and online news.* http://cnn.com

Delicious: *Social bookmarking.* http://delicious.com

DeviantArt: *Social network for artists.* http://deviantart.com

Digg: *Social news.* http://digg.com

Dopplr: *Travel social network.* http://www.dopplr.com

Drupal: *Open source CMS.* http://drupal.org

eHow: *How-to site.* http://www.ehow.com

Engadget: Gadget and technology blog.
    http://www.engadget.com

Ezine Articles: *Article hosting and distribution site.*
    http://ezinearticles.com

Facebook: *Social network.* http://facebook.com

Fast Company: *Technology and business blog.*
    http://www.fastcompany.com

Flickr: *Photo hosting site.* http://flickr.com

Flixster: *Movie social networking.* http://www.flixster.com

Fotolog: *A photoblogging network.* http://www.fotolog.com

FriendFeed: *Social network aggregator/lifestreaming service.*
    http://friendfeed.com

Friendster: *Social network.* http://www.friendster.com

Gizmodo: *Gadget blog.* http://gizmodo.com

Google: *Search engine.* http://google.com

Google AdWords: *Search advertising.*
    https://adwords.google.com

Google Analytics: *Website statistics.*
    http://www.google.com/analytics

Google Blog Search: *Blog search engine.*
    http://blogsearch.google.com

Google Groups: *Online groups.* http://groups.google.com/

Google News: *News service.* http://news.google.com

Google Video: *Video host.* http://video.google.com

Gravatar: *Globally Recognized Avatar.* http://gravatar.com

Hubpages: *Information sharing site.* http://hubpages.com

Imeem: *Music social network.* http://www.imeem.com

ItsMeJulia.com: *One of Julia Allison's domains.*
http://itsmejulia.com

iTunes: *Podcasting distribution.* http://www.apple.com/itunes

Jaiku: *Microblogging service.* http://www.jaiku.com

Joomla: *Open source CMS.* http://joomla.org

Justin.tv: *Live video streaming service.* http://www.justin.tv

Kyte: *Video hosting.* http://www.kyte.com

Last.fm: *A music-centered social network.* http://last.fm

LinkedIn: *Business social network.* http://www.linkedin.com

LiveJournal: *Free blog host and community.*
http://www.livejournal.com

Mahalo: *Information sharing site.* http://www.mahalo.com

Mashable: *Social media blog.* http://mashable.com

MediaWiki: *Open source wiki platform used for Wikipedia.*
http://www.mediawiki.org

Meetup.com: *Social network for facilitating real-life meetings.*
http://meetup.com

Metacafe: *Video hosting and sharing.*
http://www.metacafe.com

Monitor This: *Reputation management tool.*
http://alp-uckan.net/free/monitorthis

MovableType: *Blog platform.* http://movabletype.com

MyHeritage: *Genealogy social network.*
http://www.myheritage.com

MySpace: *Social network.* http://www.myspace.com

New York Times: *Newspaper and news website.*
http://nytimes.com

Ning: *A niche social network host.* http://www.ning.com

Odeo: *Podcast and vlog host.* http://odeo.com

Orkut: *Google's social network.* http://www.orkut.com

PBWiki/PBWorks: *Wiki farm.* http://pbworks.com

Photobucket: *Photo hosting and sharing.*
http://photobucket.com

Ping.fm: *Social network updating service.* http://ping.fm

PitchEngine: *Social news release builder.*
http://www.pitchengine.com

Pressitt: *Social news release builder and hosting.*
http://pressitt.com

Qik: *Mobile video hosting.* http://qik.com

Quantcast: *Website traffic statistics tracker.*
http://www.quantcast.com

Reddit: *Social news.* http://www.reddit.com

Revver: *Video sharing network.* http://revver.com

Scobleizer: *Robert Scoble's blog.* http://scobleizer.com

Scribd: *Document hosting site.* http://www.scribd.com

SisterWoman: *Social network aimed at women.*
http://sisterwoman.com

SixDegrees: *Now-defunct social network.*

Skype: *Online video phone service.* http://skype.com

Slashdot: *Technology-related social news.* http://slashdot.org

Small Business Brief: *Business-related social news.*
http://www.smallbusinessbrief.com

Squidoo: *Information sharing site.* http://www.squidoo.com

SquidWho: *Information sharing about people.*
http://www.squidwho.com

StumbleUpon: *Social bookmarking and referral site.*
http://www.stumbleupon.com

Stylefeeder: *Style-related social network and online shopping
site.* http://www.stylefeeder.com

Switched: *Gadget blog.* http://www.switched.com

Technorati: *Blog directory.* http://technorati.com

The Huffington Post: *News blog.*
http://www.huffingtonpost.com

Tip'd: *Finance-related social news.* http://tipd.com

TubeMogul: *Video tracking and analytics.*
http://tubemogul.com

Tumblr: *Blog host.* http://tumblr.com

TwitPic: *Photo hosting and sharing for Twitter.*
http://twitpic.com

Twitter: *Microblogging service.* http://twitter.com

TypePad: *Blog host.* http://www.typepad.com

Typo3: *Open source CMS.* http://typo3.org

Ubergizmo: *Gadget blog.* http://www.ubergizmo.com

Upcoming: *Local event guide.* http://upcoming.yahoo.com

UStream: *Live video streaming service.* http://www.ustream.tv

V Kontakte: *A Russian social network.* http://vkontakte.ru

WetPaint: *Website/wiki host service.* http://www.wetpaint.com

WikiHow: *How-to wiki site.* http://www.wikihow.com

Wikipedia: *User-edited encyclopedia.* http://wikipedia.org

Wired: *Technology news magazine and website.*
http://www.wired.com

WordPress: *Open source blog platform.* http://wordpress.org
or http://wordpress.com

WordPress MU: *Blogging platform for blogging communities.*
http://mu.wordpress.org

Yahoo!: *Search engine.* http://yahoo.com

Yahoo! Groups: *Group hosting.* http://groups.yahoo.com

yfrog: *Photo and video hosting and sharing for Twitter.*
http://yfrog.com

YouTube: *Video host.* http://youtube.com/

ZenHabits: *Personal development blog.* http://zenhabits.net

Sources

More resources can be found on InternetFamousBook.com

Specific Sources:

The resources mentioned here were instrumental in writing specific parts of *Internet Famous*. They are mentioned in alphabetical order, with the chapters they were used for noted.

20 Linkbaiting Techniques, *by Darren Rowse, ProBlogger. net*: http://www.problogger.net/archives/2006/09/21/20-linkbaiting-techniqes/ (Chapter 13)

A Comprehensive Guide to Using Flickr for Traffic Building and Brand Marketing, *Dosh Dosh*: http://www.doshdosh. com/comprehensive-guide-to-using-flickr-for-traffic-building/ (Chapter 8)

A Marketer's Action Guide to Microblogging, *by Chris Winfield, eMarketingandCommerce.com*: http://www. emarketingandcommerce.com/story/marketers-action-guide-microblogging (Chapter 6)

Gain a Competitive Edge by Establishing a Personal Brand, by Dan Schawbel, About.com: http://jobsearch. about.com/od/careeradviceresources/a/personalbrand.htm (Chapter 4)

HOW NOT TO: Build Your Twitter Community, by Sarah Evans, Mashable: http://mashable.com/2008/11/17/twitter-community-donts/ (Chapter 6)

How to Create Digg-Friendly Content: Cracked.com's Template, Dosh Dosh: http://www.doshdosh.com/how-to-create-digg-friendly-content/ (Chapter 15)

An Insider's Guide to Marketing On Flickr, by Rohit Bhargava, Influential Marketing Blog: http://rohitbhargava. typepad.com/weblog/2008/08/an-insiders-gui.html (Chapter 8)

Lens Building Tips Directory, by PetMemorial World, Squidoo: http://www.squidoo.com/Lens-Building-Tips-Directory (Chapter 14)

Hooked on Link Baiting, HuoMah SEO Blog: http://www. huomah.com/internet-marketing/link-building/hooked-on-link-baiting.html (Chapter 13)

MySpace Marketing Tips, Tricks, and Hints, by Luke J. Bodley, MarketingProfs: https://www.marketingprofs.com/ login/join.asp?adref=rdblk&source=%2F7%2Fmyspace-marketing-tips-bodley.asp (Chapter 7)

Marketing: The Flickr Way, Blog.SDuffyPhotography.com: http://blog.sduffyphotography.com/2008/02/21/marketing-the-flickr-way/ (Chapter 8)

B*eginners, Guide to SEO—Single Page Version*, SEOmoz: http://www.seomoz.org/article/beginners-1-page (Chapters 12 and 13)

Squidoo Traffic Tricks: (how to get more visitors and better search engine rankings for your Squidoo Lens), by MrLewisSmile, Squidoo: http://www.squidoo.com/tricks (Chapter 14)

The Secret Strategies Behind Many "Viral" Videos, by Dan Ackerman Greenberg, *TechCrunch*: http://www.techcrunch. com/2007/11/22/the-secret-strategies-behind-many-viral-videos/ (Chapter 9)

Additional Sources:

The following sources have been responsible for providing me with most of the knowledge I have about social media. While I probably couldn't cite specific articles I've found useful, if not for these sites, this book would not have been possible. I've listed them in alphabetical order for ease of reference.

Aim Clear Blog: http://www.aimclearblog.com
Bill Bolmeier: http://billbolmeier.com
Blogging Bits: http://bloggingbits.com
Blogging Tips: http://www.bloggingtips.com
Chris Brogan: http://www.chrisbrogan.com
ChrisG.com: http://www.chrisg.com
Copyblogger: http://www.copyblogger.com
Dosh Dosh: http://www.doshdosh.com
Fast Company: http://www.fastcompany.com
Fast Wonder Blog: http://fastwonderblog.com
Greg Verdino: http://gregverdino.typepad.com
Gwen Bell: http://www.gwenbell.com/blog
Hey Stephanie: http://heystephanie.com
Hubspot: http://blog.hubspot.com
Instigator Blog: http://www.instigatorblog.com
Mark Evans Tech: http://www.markevanstech.com
Marketing Pilgrim: http://www.marketingpilgrim.com
Mashable: http://mashable.com
Outspoken Media: http://outspokenmedia.com/blog
Penelope Trunk's Brazen Careerist: http://blog.
  penelopetrunk.com
Performancing.com: http://performancing.com/blog/

Podcasting.About.com: http://podcasting.about.com
PR 2.0: http://www.briansolis.com
ProBlogger: http://problogger.net
PR-Squared: http://www.pr-squared.com
ReadWriteWeb: http://www.readwriteweb.com
Robin Good's MasterNewMedia: http://www. masternewmedia.org/
SEO Book: http://www.seobook.com
SEO 2.0 SEO Blog: http://seo2.0.onreact.com
Skelliewag: http://www.skelliewag.org
Smashing Magazine: http://www.smashingmagazine.com
Social Computing Journal: http://socialcomputingjournal. com
Social Media at Work: http://socialmediaatwork.com
TechCrunch: http://www.techcrunch.com
The Future Buzz: http://thefuturebuzz.com
The Social Media Marketing Blog: http://www.scottmonty. com
Top Rank Blog: http://www.toprankblog.com
Web Strategy by Jeremiah Owyang: http://www.web-strategist.com/blog/
Wikipedia: http://wikipedia.org
Wired: http://www.wired.com